ON THE
SLOW
TRAIN

Michael Williams

arrow books

This paperback edition published by Arrow Books 2011

10 9 8 7 6 5 4 3 2 1

First published in Great Britain in 2010 by Preface Publishing
20 Vauxhall Bridge Road
London SW1V 2SA

An imprint of The Random House Group Limited

www.randomhouse.co.uk
www.prefacepublishing.co.uk

Addresses for companies within The Random House Group Limited
can be found at www.randomhouse.co.uk

The Random House Group Limited Reg. No. 954009

A CIP catalogue record for this book is available from the British Library

ISBN 978 1 84809 208 2

Mixed Sources
Product group from well-managed forests and other controlled sources
www.fsc.org Cert no. TT-COC-002139
© 1996 Forest Stewardship Council

The Random House Group Limited supports The Forest StewardshipCouncil (FSC), the leading international forest certification organisation. All our titles that are printed on Greenpeace approved FSC certified paper carry the FSC logo. Our paper procurement policy can be found at www.randomhouse.co.uk/environment

Book design by Peter Ward
Printed and bound in Great Britain by CPI Bookmarque PLC, Croydon CRO 4TD

CONTENTS

End of an era: Former Great Western Railway 'Castle' No. 5001 gets the 'right away' from Banbury on the 1.10 p.m. Paddington to Wolverhampton on the final day of regular steam working on the Birmingham line, 9 September 1962.

ON THE SLOW TRAIN

There are few things more evocative of the British landscape than the country branch line. A little engine chuffs along a single track, a few wisps of steam drifting across the fields, the sun glinting off its copper-capped chimney. There might be a couple of elderly carriages and perhaps a milk tank or a cattle truck in tow. Nobody much comes or goes on the immaculately tended platforms. Somehow here it always seems to be summer.

At least, that's how we like to imagine it. Of course, Britain's railways haven't been like this since Dr Richard Beeching, one of the great bogeymen of modern times, came along with his axe in 1963 and shut down more than 4,000 miles of track. Back then, the comedy songwriting duo Michael Flanders and Donald Swann caught the mood of the nation in their song 'Slow Train', mourning the closure of 'all those marvellous old local railway stations with their wonderful evocative names all due to be axed and done away with one by one'. 'No churns, no porter, no cat on a seat / At Chorlton-cum-Hardy or Chester-le-Street,' they sang. 'No one departs and no one arrives / From Selby to Goole, from St Erth to St Ives. / They've all passed out of our lives . . .'

Flanders and Swann's song was an elegy for the passing of a less hurried way of life. But fortunately, nearly half a century on from the publication of Beeching's *The Reshaping of British Railways,* we have learnt to love and cherish our local railways again. Slow trains on local lines offer an unrivalled way to travel around Britain in a hurried age – and they have always been more than just a way of getting from A to B. As the historian David St John Thomas observed, the local railway has always 'provided more than transport. It was always part of the district it served, with its own natural history, its own legends and folklore, a staff who were at the heart of village affairs, its stations and adjoining pubs – places for exchange of gossip, news and advice.

Luckily for us, many secondary lines didn't die at the hands of Beeching and are still here to offer the modern traveller some of the greatest journeys in Britain – and sometimes the world. There is no longer any talk of shutting Dreamingham-on-the-Marsh or Sleepytown-in-the-Wold. On the contrary, a report from the main train operating companies in 2009 urged the reopening of fourteen branch lines that had been closed by Beeching. Meanwhile passenger journeys in Britain are up by half since privatisation, and while the little old steam engines and wizened porters may be gone, many of the lines and stations that survived the cull have prospered as never before.

Even though we hear a lot about high speed rail lines expanding all over the world, the pleasures and delights of relaxed rail travel have never been more appreciated. In almost every way, the slow train journey is more pleasurable than a fast one. Think of Edward Thomas's poem 'Adlestrop', in which his express train stopped 'unwontedly' one June afternoon at an Oxfordshire country station. What he saw and heard was nothing special: the hiss of steam, an empty platform, a man clearing his throat. Yet suddenly a blackbird sang, summoning up for Thomas a profound sense of the timelessness of the English countryside. Or perhaps the most evocative slow train journey of all, Philip Larkin's 'Whitsun Weddings', written on the afternoon train from Hull: 'Not till about / One-twenty on the sunlit Saturday / Did my three-quarters empty train pull out / All windows down, all cushions hot, all sense / Of being in a hurry gone . . .'

Both poets were foreshadowing the now-fashionable concept of 'slow', which has gained momentum since the establishment of the Slow Food movement in Italy in the 1990s. Now there is even a 'Manifesto for Slow Travel', which declares that it is 'about deceleration rather than speed. The journey becomes a moment to relax, rather than a stressful interlude imposed between home and destination. Slow travel re-engineers time, transforming it into a commodity of abundance rather than scarcity.'

The great railway journeys of Britain are often the slowest – a single railcar dawdling along a Cornish branch line, a stopping train making its leisurely way through the remote heart of Wales, a vintage steam engine at the head of a Pullman train on a secondary line, its passengers enjoying a proper meal in the style of the traditional dining cars of old. How often have we peered from a local train trundling over city rooftops into back gardens and windows, catching momentary and mysterious flashes of other people's lives?

This is not a book for rivet counters or number spotters. Nor does it claim to be a history of the railways or a conventional tourist guide, although every one of the journeys can be precisely followed just as I travelled on them – simply by buying a ticket on a regular service. Rather, the book attempts to distil the flavour of Britain as glimpsed from the windows of slow trains and especially through the voices of the people in the communities they serve. Here are timeless journeys through spectacular mountains and pretty seaside villages, through gritty industrial landscapes and gently rolling hills, through city and suburbs. I have chosen them because each is special in its own right.

Since publication of the first edition of this book, the philosophy of slow travel was given an unlikely boost by the eruption of an Icelandic volcano in spring 2010. The ensuing ash cloud grounded flights across Europe, arousing fury and frustration among air passengers. But there were joys discovered by other travellers, who returned home with tales of scenic rail journeys on lines they never knew existed. As the essayist A. P. Herbert once observed 'Slow travel by train is almost the only restful experience that is left to us.' This new edition brings my journeys up to date, and includes changes suggested by readers, for which I am hugely grateful.

Settle back into the cushions, either of the train or your armchair, and enjoy the ride.

We do like to be beside the seaside: The Cornish Riviera Express
arrives at St Ives station on a summer's day in the 1930s.
Although Beeching wanted to close it, the line was reprieved
and is flourishing again today.

CHAPTER ONE

THE 09.05 TO ST IVES — THE LINE THEY COULDN'T CLOSE

St Erth to Lelant, Carbis Bay and St Ives

Everybody has dreamt of a land where the sun always shines and has never proved harmful, where it is always warm, but never enervating, where we may bathe in the winter and take active exercise in the summer. We had to have a name for this Elysium, so we called it the Cornish Riviera

This morning I am officially standing in Paradise. Well, actually I'm on the platform of St Erth station in Cornwall, the remotest junction in the most westerly part of England, with the Great Western Railway's famous 1934 guidebook *The Cornish Riviera* in my pocket, from which this quote is taken. It's a bit chilly even on a July morning in this Elysium, but we must believe what we are told because the book is published with the imprimatur of 'Sir James Milne, General Manager, Paddington Station, London'. As every schoolchild with any knowledge of the railway system knows, GWR stands for God's Wonderful Railway.

But there is another special reason for being here today. Michael Flanders and Donald Swann proved remarkably prophetic in their song 'Slow Train'. Ultimately, most of the little stations and lines they sang about closed down, but there was a major exception – the branch from this unspoilt little Victorian station to St Ives, seven miles from here along the Hayle estuary. 'From Selby to Goole,' they sang, 'from St Erth to St Ives. / They've all passed out of our lives.' But they didn't all disappear, as it turns out. The little cerise-coloured Class 150 diesel railcar humming in the bay platform is proof of how much has changed in nearly half a century since Beeching, and just how wrong the former BR chairman got it. Not only has it outlived the good chairman, it is one of the few rural branch lines in the UK to make money.

These days, with St Ives transformed from a backward pilchard-fishing village to a cool international resort, with its own branch of the Tate Gallery, the railway has resumed the same central place in the town's life as it had when it was built in 1877. If only Flanders and Swann could have lived to see it. Passenger numbers have more than doubled in less than ten years. And not only that; we are in for a visual treat. The St Ives Bay line may be only four and a quarter miles long, but many regard it as the most scenic short railway in Europe.

But first a flapjack and coffee served by the homely lady in the privately run buffet by St Erth's little bay platform. A notice on the wall proclaims it to be No. 4 in the *Guardian*'s list of Britain's top ten railway station cafes. Pelargoniums and petunias tumble from hanging baskets outside and there are lupins and zinnias in the platform tubs. At one time I might have arrived here aboard the most famous train in the land: the Cornish Riviera Express. Leaving Paddington sharp at 10.30 in the morning behind a burnished King Class locomotive, all shining brass, copper and Brunswick green, the Cornish Riviera was the one train above all that inspired young boys to become railway enthusiasts – probably first encountering it on a summer Saturday, trailing tin buckets and spades along the platform, heading for sunny destinations such as St Ives, Falmouth, Newquay and Weymouth. Until the end of steam in the 1960s, I might not even have needed to get off at St Erth to change for St Ives. The 'Limited', as it was known, was so busy it ran in several portions, including one direct to St Ives. The Great Western's managers reserved the company's very best Dreadnought coaches for the train, with the biggest windows, the widest aisles and the plumpest cushions the company possessed. I have a faded 1950s picture of the Paddington train, ten coaches long, being huffed and puffed along the branch by three little Prairie Tanks – one at the front and two pushing at the back. Boys in their best blazers and girls in freshly ironed Ladybird dresses fill the carriages, waiting to jump straight onto the beach, which sits alongside St Ives station.

These days, rail travel is not quite so commodious. The current operator of the line, First Great Western, has retained a decent enough respect for its heritage to keep the Cornish Riviera title, along with the names of the other great Cornish trains of the past – the Royal Duchy and the Golden Hind. But these trains are just normal services – bog-standard high speed trains indistinguishable from any other. But there remains one service that can match up to the glamour of the old Great Western in its heyday. I have arrived at St Erth this morning aboard the Night Riviera, the last remaining sleeping-car train running entirely within England. Like the St Ives branch, this too nearly died, when withdrawal was proposed in 2005. But it was saved when passengers organised an 8,000-name protest petition. It may not have had one of C B Collett's famous Kings or Castles on the front, but as I set off on my journey from Paddington to St Erth last night I couldn't deny a quiet thrill (not often found on the British main line these days) when I saw a powerful locomotive backing down onto the train – a rare thing on a passenger service nowadays. This was the Class 57 diesel *Tintagel Castle*, burnished up in the green livery of the old Great Western. Sentiment dies hard at Paddington, even in the modern corporate world. I got chatting with the driver, who told me that the forty-year-old *Tintagel Castle* had been built only a decade or so after the last steam Castles had emerged from the Swindon works – and so the provenance of locomotives named after castles on this line has been almost unbroken since the first ones were built in 1923. Perhaps the only difference is that the elderly diesels used on the Night Riviera these days – unlike the products of Swindon in the steam age – are prone to breaking down. But last night the journey on the 23.45 from Paddington was faultless, and I slept soundly.

My connection to St Ives is waiting cosily tucked into the bay platforms, a little lower than the main line, as if in deference to the grown-up expresses that race by, though in reality this is to accommodate the gradient of the branch line as it falls away northwards towards the Hayle estuary. Could there be a more perfect little station? Virtually unchanged since it was built in 1852, with granite buildings, wooden canopies and semaphore signals (authentically 'lower quadrant' in the GWR style), it looks for all the world as though it has been transplanted from a model railway exhibition. With half an hour to go till departure, I buy the local morning paper, the *Western Morning News*, whose head-line reads, 'Future bright for delightful railway lines'. Although the future is less bright, I think, for newspapers like this one, who are undergoing their own Beeching axe all over the country as declining circulations put the parish pump out of business and the Internet takes over. Who would have bet, back in 1963, that the St Ives line would prosper, yet newspapers, like this once-mighty daily paper of Devon and Cornwall would face oblivion?

'There were few pleasures in England that could beat the small three-coach branch-line train like this one from St Erth to St Ives,' wrote Paul Theroux in his 1983 book *The Kingdom by the Sea*. 'You knew a branch line with your eyes shut.' My Class 150 unit is in authentic branch line tradition, using hand-me-down vehicles that have seen better times elsewhere. It wears the livery of Arriva Trains Wales and is well off its home territory, but is comfortable enough and the windows are clean. The signal clatters, and we are off down the branch, slowing to pick up the 'staff' from the signalman. Funny how the old terms persist – the branch is operated on what is still known as a 'one engine in steam' basis, which means that so long as our driver has the old-fashioned baton, no other trains can gain access to the line.

A family of shelducks and a couple of tiny egrets flap away as the train pootles along the edge of the salt flats. But the rural spell is shattered at the next station, Lelant Saltings, when literally hundreds of people push their way aboard. 'Have you ever seen the state of the roads in St Ives?' the conductor explains. 'There are buses and vans scraping each other's mirrors off and running over the toes of the tourists. It's gridlock hell. So a lot of people head for the park-and-ride up here.' And off he goes, his ticket machine whirring, selling four-pound fares to people who probably don't travel on trains from one year to the next.

But I have to interrupt him for the request stop at Lelant – an original little wooden wayside station, its chocolate-and-cream Great Western Railway-style paintwork reflected in the clear tidal waters of the Hayle, which laps at the edge of the tracks. The building was long ago sold off as a private residence, and its owner, a large red-headed man called Peter Jeggo, is sitting in the garden watching the birds across the bay. This is one of Britain's greatest ports of call for migrating flocks, where dunlins, sanderlings, ring-tailed plovers and bar-tailed godwits drop in to take their supper. Jeggo, now retired from his job in London as a supermarket operations manager, sells Cornish cream teas and offers the benefit of his knowledge of the history of the line to anyone who cares to listen.

'Look at this.' He takes me indoors to show me the original plans for the station, framed on the wall. 'These date from the year before the line was built in 1877. There's a first-class ladies waiting room, a second- and third-class one and a general waiting room. Can you imagine? Three separate waiting rooms in a tiny station in the middle of nowhere?'

The building of the line was a grand gesture by a consortium of the Great Western, Bristol and Exeter and West Cornwall railways, who saw in the failed mines and uncertain fisheries of St Ives little prospect of success but were persuaded in the vague hope the town might become a tourist resort. The directors of the railway put on a brave show. On the morning of 24 March 1877 the directors' train, consisting of a saloon and six composite carriages drawn by the locomotive *Elephant*, left Penzance station to make the inaugural journey to St Ives. According to the *Cornwall Telegraph,* bonfires were lit, tar barrels were set ablaze along the coast and a national holiday was declared. But not everyone in Lelant was happy, particularly about the behaviour of the navvies who built the line. The newspaper reported that there was 'drunkenness, to a lamentable extent. Last Sunday, from about half past two in the afternoon till late at night, drunken men were rambling about the roads much to the disgust of the decent inhabitants.' To make matters worse, a number of skulls were found along the course of the line, with jawbones full of teeth which the navvies extracted to keep as talismans against getting the toothache themselves.

'And did you know,' Jeggo tells me, pouring coffee into his railway-monogrammed mug, 'that the St Ives line has a special claim to fame? It was the very last in Britain to be built to the broad gauge.' Even though the great engineer was voted in a recent poll the second-greatest Briton of all time, Isambard Kingdom Brunel made a spectacular error in his insistence on plumping for a different gauge from all other railways in the land. Brunel rejected George Stephenson's sensible gauge of 4 feet 8½ inches, which went back to the days of the horse tramways and approximates to the width of a horse's backside. Brunel wanted to be bigger and better than Stephenson, and chose a gauge of 7 feet ¼ inch, half as wide again. His reasons were eccentric, complaining that the ride on Stephenson's Liverpool and Manchester Railway was so rough that he couldn't draw a freehand circle, and he claimed that the wider gauge would lead to fewer derailments. Brunel in his arrogance believed that the other railways would fall in with his ideas, but the Great Western was forced to recant and scrap thousands of locomotives at vast cost when Parliament decreed that the standard gauge should prevail. By 1892 it was gone, though why the St Ives promoters were still building the 7 feet ¼ inch gauge in 1877 when other parts of the system were already being converted back again is a mystery Peter Jeggo and I don't have time to discuss, since I have to catch the next train north-west. There won't be another for hours because the intensive timetable on the single track between St Erth and St Ives during the main part of the day means the trains are too busy to stop in a backwater like Lelant.

From virtually sea level here, the line swings with a squealing of wheels around the headland and begins to climb. Across the salt marshes you can see the wharves and warehouses of Hayle, once dominated by the huge foundries set up by the blacksmith John Harvey in 1779, which produced some of the greatest beam engines in the world, employing some of the giants from the age of steam, including Richard Trevithick. Times are harder now: Harvey's shut down in 1989 and the creamery followed soon after. But things have always been tough in this part of Cornwall. In the book *Branch Lines to Falmouth, Helston and St Ives* by Victor Mitchell and Keith Smith is a picture of a Great Western Railway emigrant's ticket to Liverpool, price twenty-five shillings – life savings for some poor wretch who had no alternative but to escape to the New World.

As the train reaches the mouth of the river it turns north along the cliffs above the open sea, with the whole vast sweep of the estuary, glistening today with that special azure light that has brought generations of artists to St Ives. Fix your eye on the horizon and you can see Godrevy Lighthouse, perched in the spray on a wave-thrashed rock. This was the inspiration for Virginia Woolf's famous 1927 novel *To the Lighthouse*. Long before she became part of the Bloomsbury set, Woolf spent many happy holidays as a child near here playing on nearby Upton Towans beach, although in the novel she located the lighthouse in the Hebrides.

Hikers stride by on the nearby South West Coast Path as the train continues above the vast tidal beach of Porth Kidney Sands – miles of deserted dunes which train passengers have all to themselves since the builders of the railway cleverly cut them off from the nearby roads. Drivers in the slow-moving traffic on the parallel A3074 barely get a glimpse of the coast all the way to St Ives. Then the train dives into a deep cutting across the headland of Carrack Gladden, whose Cornish name translates as 'rocks on the brink' and which drips with heather and rhododendrons, before reaching the summit of the line just before Carbis Bay, where I get off to dip my toes in the water alongside the families playing on the beach.

At the turn of the nineteenth century, the managers of the Great Western Railway had a genius for developing bleak little Cornish towns, where the mines were failing and the fish stocks running out, into thriving seaside resorts for the growing middle classes, who were happy to fork out a family fare from Paddington for two weeks of balmy Cornish weather each summer, to stay in hotels developed by the railway. It's hard to imagine, as I sip a gin and tonic in the Edwardian surroundings of the terrace of the Carbis Bay Hotel, that near here was the giant Wheal Providence tin mine, where hundreds of men, women and children once laboured in appalling and dangerous conditions. Not much danger here these days, and passengers concerned about safety will be reassured by the photograph of a notice on the bar wall. 'Conversion of gauge,' it reads. 'This is to certify that the line between St Erth and Carbis Bay is ready and the ordinary working of trains between these points can be resumed on Monday May 22nd 1892. Signed, Albert Harris, Traffic Inspector.'

These days Carbis Bay is very genteel – no Blackpool this. It's full of nice families from Wandsworth or Wimbledon, trying to recreate wholesome holidays of the past, although there's a fair chance visitors will encounter the many Germans who come here to pay homage to the novelist Rosamund Pilcher, who was born near the village. In Britain she is regarded as a bit Mills and Boon, but her most famous novel *The Shell Seekers* has almost cult status in Germany, where many of her stories have been adapted for television. If you are lucky you may arrive on St James's Day, when once every five years people flock to an obelisk erected nearby by John Knill, an eighteenth-century mayor of St Ives. Under the terms of his will, ten girls of under fourteen years of age, dressed in white and accompanied by a fiddler and two widows, dance for one and a quarter hours while they sing the hymn 'All People That on Earth Do Dwell' and a song imploring 'Virgins fair and pure as fair to fly St Ives and all her treasures, fly her soft voluptuous pleasures.'

I have the 'voluptuous pleasures' of St Ives in mind as I resume my journey to the town, across the four seventy-eight-foot-high stone arches of the Carbis Viaduct, and past the old baulking house, from where a 'huer' would cross a special bridge over the line to watch from the headland for shoals of pilchards. He would use a hand-held signalling device to the men in the boats below as they set out their huge seine net. At one time pilchards were more important than passengers here. In the first twelve months of the line's operation, the takings from St Ives station were: 'passengers £1874; fish £5245'. 'Once,' according to the GWR's Cornish Riviera guide of 1934, 'seventy-five million were netted in one day and St Ives was £60,000 the richer. It is, however, a precarious business. The pilchards come in millions or not at all, and of recent years the huers have scanned the waters in vain for many weary months.' It quotes a story of St Ives men whipping a hake through the town to warn its fellows not to touch the pilchards.

Too late to whip a hake or anything else through St Ives these days – the humble pilchard became a victim of fashion as well as overfishing. Although a clever marketing exercise has rebranded the pilchard the 'Cornish sardine' and repositioned it from the cat's plate to barbecues on smart Islington patios, it has been too late for St Ives. The canneries have closed and what remains of the industry has moved down the coast to Newlyn.

On the last stage of its journey down the hill into St Ives, the train passes through a heavily wooded cutting. When Paul Theroux came this way in 1983, he wrote, 'There was never any question that I was on a branch line train, for it was only on these trains that the windows were brushed by the trees that grew close to the tracks. It was possible to tell from the sounds at the windows – the branches pushed the glass like mops and brooms.' You might expect from all the grandeur of the journey that the arrival into the town would be especially splendid. And so it is – in one sense. As the train emerges from the cutting and over the Porthminster Viaduct the view is heart-stopping. Here is a panorama of the whole bay with its silvery sands, the twisty streets of the town like barley sugar and the headland, all bathed in the pearly light that has inspired generations of artists.

But wait. Where is the station to match the unspoilt Victorian charm of the town? Sadly, the bulldozers reduced it to a pile of rubble in 1971, just six years before the line's centenary. All that remains to greet the modern passenger is a prefabricated bus shelter and a single concrete platform with an automatic ticket machine marooned in the middle of a car park. All the more poignant is the fact that the original granite walls around the perimeter of the old station still stand – a reminder of how extensive the tracks here once were. It was the complete country terminus – four roads, a solid little booking office with canopy. There was a goods office and a little engine shed, a couple of camping coaches and a siding for the trucks that would speed the fish up to market along with that other perishable Cornish staple, the broccoli harvest, now also sadly lost to the area.

Was the demolition retribution by British Railways managers for the refusal to let them shut the line? I am about to meet the man who can tell me, since he is arriving on the afternoon train. 'You'll recognise me,' Richard Burningham explains, 'because I'll be the only person getting out of the carriages wearing a suit.' It is even a pinstriped one – appropriate in a way, since Burningham is in a sense the 'Fat Controller' for the line. As the representative of the Devon and Cornwall Rail Partnership, he is responsible for the sustenance and development of all the railway lines west of Exeter, spearheading an alliance of train operators, passenger

14

groups and local authorities. 'Hmm,' he says, squinting at the map of St Ives at the end of the platform. 'We could do with a better one of these.'

We retire to the Pedn-Olva Hotel over the road and join elderly ladies in Lloyd Loom chairs in the lounge overlooking the bay for a pot of tea. Since British Railways applied its scorched-earth policy to the station, the hotel is now the town's closest thing to a railway refreshment room. Burningham is passionate about the lines in his charge and has given me a faded copy of a press release from the Ministry of Transport dated 20th September 1966. Buried inside the officialese is the story of how the line was snatched back to safety from under the nose of Beeching's executioners by the Labour transport minister Barbara Castle. Castle was one of the most notorious or most effective transport ministers in history, depending on your view. She introduced the breathalyser, the 70 mph speed limit on motorways and car seat belts, but also presided over 2,050 miles of Beeching cuts in a betrayal of Prime Minister Harold Wilson's pledge to reverse them.

Even before Beeching, BR was swinging the axe in the West Country, Burningham tells me. The line from Gwinear Road to Helston shut in 1962. The Plymouth to Launceston route followed in the same year, though the piskies sabotaged the plans of BR managers in London by stranding a train at Tavistock in a snowstorm, preventing the closure of the line. Beeching was ruthless, set on obliterating almost every branch line west of Plymouth, including Bere Alston–Callington, Bodmin–Wadebridge–Padstow, Liskeard–Looe, Lostwithiel–Fowey, Okehampton–Bude, Okehampton–Padstow – and St Erth–St Ives. Flanders and Swann could have written an entire song using just the names of the stations on the main line from Plymouth to Penzance that passed from the timetable in 1964 – Boublebois, Grampound Road, Chacewater, Scorrier, Gwinear Road and Marazion.

But Mrs Castle clearly had a soft spot for St Ives as well as the little line from Liskeard to Looe, eastwards along the coast. You can hear the forthright northern tones coming through the faded typescript.

I have refused to close the branch lines serving St Ives and Looe in Cornwall. In spite of the financial saving to the railways, it just wouldn't have made sense to transfer heavy holiday traffic to roads which couldn't cope with it. Nor would expensive road improvements have been the answer. At St Ives, these would have involved destroying the whole character of the town. It would be the economics of bedlam to spend vast sums only to create greater inconvenience.

'You know,' says Burningham, 'this line is probably the most scenic in Europe, if not the world. Just imagine if it hadn't been saved,' he says, pointing out the huge crowds getting off the train over the road. To see what might have happened at St Ives you only have to listen to the words of the historian David St John Thomas, who travelled on the last train on the neighbouring Helston branch.

Platform, refreshment room, approach road milled with onlookers. Cameras flashed as a party of boys in top hats laid a wreath on the locomotive and a sandwich board mockingly declared 'the end is at hand' . . . the crowd sang 'Auld Lang Syne' as the engine exploded detonators and the train disappeared into the night. Nobody hurried to leave; people talked of the old days, of when everybody came and went by train, of father telling how he had helped build the line, of how uncle had lost money on it, of grandson aged seven who had taken his first train trip that afternoon. From Monday anyone coming from London could no longer change from the Cornish Riviera Express straight into a waiting train at Gwinear Road; many local residents would have to change cars or change jobs.

Lucky the redoubtable Mrs Castle stayed the axe at both Looe and St Ives. She clearly repented later in life of some of her more draconian actions, and Burningham shows me a poignant note that the ninety-one-year-old politician sent to him on 9 May 2001, shortly before she died. 'Dear Richard,' she writes,

I am very sorry not to be able to be with you today but unfortunately a slight injury has put me out of action for a few weeks. I would have enjoyed immensely helping you to celebrate the anniversary of the opening of the line from Liskeard to Looe, which passes through some of the most beautiful country in England. I have an almost maternal feeling for it since I was able in the 1960s to save it from the slaughter of the innocence [sic]. Long may it and you continue to flourish.

And so does St Ives on this sunny day, with the town's five species of gulls, identified by the famous ornithologist W H Hudson, squawking overhead and children sucking cornets and foraging in rock pools. Hudson was a frequent visitor to the town, staying in a cottage in Lelant. Where once the train brought in lumps of rock for Barbara Hepworth's sculptures, clay for Bernard Leach's potter's wheel and canvases for its other great son, Ben Nicholson, now their disciples pour in to queue outside the hugely successful Tate St Ives and to dine in the town's smart new restaurants. There are still pasties and clotted cream galore to be found around town, but the new St Ives set are more likely to be found eating curried Cornish monkfish in the Porthminster Café, a former deckchair repair hut transformed into one of the trendiest restaurants in the West Country. And even though the old station has gone, the ghosts of the railway are to be found everywhere in the town. In the Tate I buy a postcard of a 1960s painting by the self-taught artist Tom Early of a single-coach train crossing the Porthminster viaduct. Farther along the quay, in the St Ives Museum, among the dusty jumble of ephemera so typical of small-town museums, is a section on the local railway. Here is the nameplate from Castle Class No. 5006, named *Tregenna Castle* after the Great Western Railway's famous hotel in the town – the first railway hotel to be opened away from a major terminus and purely for the benefit of the holiday trade. The hotel flourishes today, although the suites where elderly dowagers from Belgravia once came to take the sun have been turned into holiday apartments for families. The locomotive, the museum tells us, was withdrawn in 1962 having run a total of 1,809,297 miles. 'She hauled the Cheltenham Flyer, which achieved a record time on the journey Swindon to Paddington – 77¼ miles in 56 minutes 47 seconds on 6th June 1932 – thereby becoming the world's fastest train.' Here too is a group portrait of the 'Staff of St Ives Railway station, c.1955', which tells us everything about why the St Ives line went into decline. In the centre sits Mr M J Rich, the stationmaster, with his splendidly braided hat, along with six porters, two signalmen, four clerks, an engine cleaner and a carriage cleaner. There are twenty-three of them in all. No wonder Beeching took fright when he looked at the books.

But have things gone too far the other way? Jeremy Joslin thinks so. I meet the president of the Hayle Chamber of Commerce in the Badger Inn at Lelant on my way back to St Erth and Paddington. The old inn was once a favourite of the Stephens, Virginia Woolf's family, when they came on the train from Paddington for their summer holidays. Joslin is one of the line's most fervent supporters and dreams one day of taking it back into local ownership. 'The people up at Paddington run it like any other railway. But the problem that Beeching identified is still there. The line is just too seasonal. I'd put bums on seats in the winter by running steam trains and dining cars. One of our biggest supporters is the local vicar and he'd love to do weddings on board the trains.' There's a gleam in his eye as he talks of plans to bring in low-cost trains powered by a flywheel and distribute goods to the shops in St Ives using mini-containers that would fit onto specially adapted motorbikes.

Will there be change? Maybe. But the truth is that the St Ives Bay line, with its summer trains packed to the doors, is quite successful as it is, thank you. As I squeeze aboard, joining exhausted but happy families heading back to the park-and-ride, I wonder: can there be any other branch line in the land whose future has been secured by the motor car?

High drama: A 'Black Five' and a 'Jubilee' double-head
the Waverley Express over the Ribblehead viaduct, c. 1958.
The picture is by Eric Treacy, Bishop of Wakefield,
one of the line's most devoted enthusiasts.

CHAPTER TWO

THE 15.03 FROM CARLISLE TO THE ROOF OF ENGLAND

Carlisle to Leeds, via Appleby, Dent, Ribblehead and Settle

Eat your heart out, Trans-Siberian. Take the slow line, Orient Express. This seventy-three-mile railway from Carlisle over the roof of England to West Yorkshire is up there with the grandest and most thrilling train journeys in the world. Blasted across the bleak and unforgiving limestone and black marble of the Pennines, this former Anglo-Scottish main line was the final truly grand gesture of Victorian railway building. It was the last to be constructed using the sheer brute muscle of men working with just pickaxes and dynamite. Hundreds died in the six and and a half years it took to construct the 'Long Drag' across the great wilderness of northern England. Many perished from accidents, cold and disease in the unforgiving terrain. Some simply hanged themselves in despair as floods and storms swept away their handiwork. This was truly the *Götterdämmerung* of the railways.

Ironically, this – possibly the craziest – enterprise of the Victorian railway mania need not have been built at all. Back in 1869, when the Settle and Carlisle was begun, there were two perfectly good main lines to take passengers to Scotland – the London and North Western route from Euston via Crewe, and the Great Northern route from King's Cross via York. But back amid the mahogany and crystal of the Midland Railway's boardroom in Derby, James Allport, the company's general manager, was restless. The Midland was making a fortune trundling coal, beer, iron and bricks around the Midlands. But this 'Fat Controller' of his age wanted something more daring, more glamorous. He'd already marched his forces into London, planting the magnificent Gothic towers of St Pancras station as a taunt to his rivals along the Euston Road. And so the order went out: 'Hang the terrain. Don't bother me with trivia! Just build me a railway to Scotland that will be better than all our competitors, by God!' Allport was a religious man and his vision was messianic in the true Victorian sense. So a pencil line was drawn over the mountains between Leeds and the Borders, and 6,000 men spent the next six and a half years hacking their way across them.

Since this is to be a journey of superlatives, it seems appropriate that I should be standing as dusk falls on the platform at Dent station in Cumbria, after arriving up the line from Carlisle. A notice underneath the lamp declares that this is the HIGHEST MAIN LINE STATION IN ENGLAND, 1,150 FEET ABOVE SEA LEVEL. Once there would have been a roaring fire in the waiting room and a cheery porter with a fob watch ready to announce the time of the next London connection. Tonight, there is nobody to be seen on this unstaffed platform. As the lights of the train from which I have disembarked disappear into the blackness and all I can hear is the eerie rush of a gill running beneath the tracks, it is perfectly easy, on this bleak autumn evening, to imagine I might be the last soul left alive in the universe.

Still, it's thanks to the doggedness of local folk that the line is running at all. Back in 1981, British Rail decided the entire railway must close because the 440-yard Ribblehead viaduct, striding heroically across the wastes of Batty Moss, was too expensive to repair. Never mind that with its 24 arches, 104 feet high, held up by 1.5 million bricks faced with limestone it was one of the engineering marvels of the Victorian age. No matter that it had a Grade II * listing from English Heritage and that its domination of the landscape is every bit as great as that of Stonehenge, the estimated £6 million cost of repair was deemed uneconomic by the BR accountants in London. But they didn't reckon with the 25,000 people (and a dog) who put up objections. After a six-year campaign, the bureaucrats, worn down by the gritty folk of North Yorkshire, backed off. It would be a reckless official indeed who ever tangled with this hardy breed of locals to propose its closure again.

My journey to Dent began on the 15.03 from Carlisle to Leeds, a spartan little two-car Class 158 diesel unit, all vinyl and worn seats, typical of British Rail in the 1980s, when passengers were reckoned to get in the way of the real business – closing down railways. These days it is operated by Northern Rail, a consortium of the Dutch State Railways and a company called Serco, more famous perhaps for operating detention centres and speed cameras on Britain's highways. This may seem a surreal commercial arrangement in this heartland of traditional England, but such is the nature of the modern privatised railway.

The Express Sprinter unit – a misnomer if ever there was one – sits wheezing and guttering, and shooting clouds of blue fumes over Carlisle's Platform 1. At least the heaters are working full blast, though the windows could do with a clean, and one of them has so much condensation between the double glazing it looks as though there's a pea-souper outside. It's a far cry from the splendour of the first train on the opening of the line on May Day 1876. James Allport had been to America and met a young carriage manufacturer called George Mortimer Pullman (the name was yet to pass into the lexicon as a synonym for luxury). Allport ordered two of George Mortimer's new-fangled Pullman cars for the Settle and Carlisle and opened up a new era of luxurious rail travel, with flushing lavatories and sprung bogies which gave a ride like silk. 'Altogether magnificent,' pronounced the correspondent of the *Railway News*.

> All the seats are covered in Utrecht velvet, while the whole of the woodwork is of American walnut, with much tasteful gilding and painting. Numerous other comforts, great and little, including a system of warming by hot

water pipes, and abundance of curtains, and lavatories for both ladies and gentlemen, raise travelling in the Pullman Palace train from a fatigue to a positive pleasure.

But it's not the life of a Victorian sybarite I'm thinking of as our little train rattles over the points to leave the Newcastle line at Petteril Bridge Junction for the relentless ascent for the next fifty miles along the spectacular landscapes of the Eden Valley. For the moment this is gentle country, all fruit trees and pasture in the summer. But it was a different story for the line's first surveyor, a lanky young Tasmanian called Charles Stanley Sharland, who set out to walk the entire route before it was built, armed with just a compass, theodolite and a few basic instruments. Just as Robert Stephenson had waded across bog and fell to determine the course of the first passenger railway from Liverpool to Manchester fifty years before, so Sharland and a couple of assistants trudged through the mountains, sometimes trapped by snow in lonely fellside inns for weeks on end. Unlike Stephenson, the Tasmanian's brief was to prepare for the construction of not a local line, but a state-of-the-art main trunk route. There had to be no gradient steeper than 1 in 100, which meant that three and a half miles of expensive tunnels and dozens of viaducts were needed. To this day the Settle and Carlisle is the only fully fledged main line in the world running through such mountainous country. But the unfortunate Sharland did not live to see his work completed. He died at the age of twenty-six, his health broken by his efforts.

The young surveyor might have been proud though to see the spruce little wayside stations built in 'Derby Gothic' style by the architect I H Saunders. We nearly lost them, but thankfully they were reopened in 1986 after a closure of sixteen years when the threat to the line was finally lifted. Armathwaite, Langwathby, Lazonby and Kirkoswald – you almost have to pronounce their names with a Cumbrian lilt as we climb the valley of the Eden, with the river full and fast flowing, never far from our side. On our left are Long Meg and her daughters, an ancient circle dating back 4,500 years – the original sixty-six daughters having been turned to stone after sacrilegious acts on the sabbath, becoming what is now the second-largest stone circle in Britain. The skyline for miles to the left is dominated by Cross Fell, the highest point in the Pennines at 2,930 feet. The white dome on the top of Great Dun Fell, the summit of the Pennine Way, is as sinister as it actually looks, since if we ever scramble our nuclear deterrent, the button will be pushed as a result of an early warning from here. The distant fells on the horizon to the right, looking like a giant iced cake, are those of Ullswater in the Lake District.

I know all this because I have been joined on my journey south from Carlisle by a retired pharmacist called Tony Iles, a volunteer Friend of the Settle and Carlisle, who spends his days riding the trains pointing out the sights to anyone who is interested. There's clearly nobody more passionate about the line than Tony, who wears a maroon S & C jumper, and along with the rest of the Friends fought British Rail and successive transport ministers between 1984 and 1989 to save it from closure. He tells me,

> It was a devious strategy they deployed on all the lines they wanted to shut. You reduce the trains, cut back on the maintenance, drive away the passengers, and then concoct some story about repairs, claiming the line is not worth keeping open. After we finally beat them, it turned out the cost of repairing Ribblehead Viaduct was nothing like what BR claimed. And passenger numbers shot up from 98,000 a year to half a million.

These days Network Rail is spending more than £100 million on the line – not to improve its passenger services, which are still a mere five through trains a day – but, ironically, because of the decline of another traditional industry – coal. Much of the fuel for Britain's coal-fired power stations is imported in massive container ships through the port of Hunterston on the west coast of Scotland. It is routed south in vast 1,250-tonne trains over the S & C, securing the line's future for the foreseeable future. But you can't please everybody. 'The enthusiasts complain that the track is *too* smooth and the *tiddly-tat* of the old fashioned line has been eliminated,' says Tony. 'And now they're moaning that the old semaphore signals are going to be replaced by modern colour-light ones! You can't have it both ways. A lot of people think we're privately owned by a preservation society. I tell you, no heritage buffs could afford the investment to run something like this.'

We break off as we halt at a station rather more splendid than the rest. This is Appleby, the only staffed station on the line between Carlisle and Settle. No better spot to break your journey than this unspoilt medieval farming town, watched over by its castle, the little cafes and shops on the high street as far away as it is possible to get from modern corporate Britain. The mock-Gothic brick station with its mullioned windows and paintwork on the ornate bargeboards, newly painted in the crimson colours of the Midland Railway, is immaculate in the unweathered fashion of a Hornby toy train layout.

Appleby station is the fiefdom of Anne Ridley, the station supervisor, a jolly blonde who greets me like a long-lost friend. How nice! Since she does not know me, it is clear she must welcome all the passengers who alight at this isolated town in similar fashion. There's plenty of time for a natter before the next train arrives, although Anne has been busy this morning, she tells me, feeding the sheep at her farm in the village of Kirkby Thore, along the line. 'I've also been cleaning the toilets and dusting and polishing the waiting room, as well as doing the ticket office accounts.' She smiles. 'And then there's my husband. He doesn't always come last, though it may sometimes sound like it! Come and have a coffee,' she says. With its neat pot plants and wood-burning stove, Anne's waiting room is a homely place. The polished limestone floor is so shiny, you could eat your dinner off it, as Alan Bennett – also from this part of the world and a leading figure in heading off the line's closure – might say.

Anne has been queen of Appleby station for nine years, after swapping her career in the police for 'the best job in the world', and works in shifts with her staff of two. She also organises the refreshments for all the trains, sourcing her food from local farmers' wives. 'I'm a people person, you see, and I love it here.' Her customers are not just sightseers doing the Yorkshire Dales, but locals heading up and down the valleys – farmers off for tough interviews with their bank managers in Leeds and their teenage children heading for the (relatively) bright lights of Carlisle. 'Honestly, what would they do without us? It's unbelievable – you have to take two buses to get into Carlisle, and it takes hours.'

As I wait for the next train south, it is hard to imagine that the sleeping-car trains from London to Scotland once stopped here, in the middle of nowhere. Nightshirted and nightcapped figures would lean out of the carriages in the small hours wondering where on earth they were. But Appleby station has another, albeit poignant, claim to fame, commemorated by a little plaque on the platform and a shrine of memorabilia in the corner of Anne Ridley's immaculate waiting room. Back in 1978, the Right Reverend Eric Treacy, Bishop of Wakefield, lifelong railway enthusiast and celebrated railway photographer, suffered a fatal heart attack while photographing trains on the down platform. The 'Railway Bishop' was devoted to the Settle and Carlisle, describing it as one of the three wonders of northern England, along with York Minster and Hadrian's Wall. His memorial service, held on the platform, was attended by 3,000 people, including six bishops – and three steam locomotives. As Anne waves me off, I notice that the station clock, made by Potts of Leeds in 1870, has stopped at twenty to five. Goodness knows for how long. But it seems appropriate somehow.

It is appropriate too that I should buy a slice of home-made 'Stem Ginger Shortbread handmade in Dalefoot Farm' from

Anne's trolley on the train. Delicious. I imagine Dalefoot Farm somewhere out there in this chilly autumn countryside – remote maybe, but with the Aga ever warm and the sheepdog curled up at its side. I ask the guard about the weather up at Ribblehead as we climb relentlessly through an increasingly bleak landscape. 'Just like it generally is – cold and getting colder,' he tells me. ''Twas much worse at one time, winter after winter. Just watch you wrap up well when you get off! It's the wind that's the trouble,' he says, telling how icy gusts coming straight off the North Sea would blow the coal off the fireman's shovel in steam days. 'Then there were the chap whose hat was blown off a train on the Ribblehead Viaduct, sucked right through an arch and ended up back on the train on the other side. One day up at Garsdale station, the wind caught the turntable and it spun like a top for an hour before they could get the loco off.' Folk memory still recalls the bitter winter of 1947 when the line was closed for eight weeks, buried under twelve feet of snow. Even bonfires were unable to clear the rails. The line was shut again in 1962, when the Edinburgh to London express was stuck in the snow for five days. Passengers lived off tea and biscuits till they were rescued.

Even at the height of summer this is a wind-lashed landscape of sparse heather, peat bog and raw limestone pavement. Now on this late autumn afternoon we could be anywhere north of Reykjavik. The train's underfloor engines take on a more determined note as we climb through Kirkby Stephen, once grand enough to have a first-class waiting room. Now it is unstaffed, but with a plaque saying that Prince Charles unveiled the restored station buildings and a little notice on one of the doors proclaiming BIBLE VOICE. This marks a tradition going back more than a century in which local vicars came to these remote stations, carrying altar cloth, chalice and a portable organ, taking advantage of the railway to spread the word of God in remote places. These days, a local couple, Martin and Liz Thompson, run a short-wave

Christian radio station from here, broadcasting the word to remote villages around the world, including to India in Hindi. There are other radio connections, too, since nearby is the birthplace of Lord Thomas Wharton, who in the seventeenth century wrote the words of 'Lillibullero', the much-loved signature tune of the BBC World Service.

Kirkby Stephen is a handsome town built of the local 'brockram' stone – a mix of sandstone and limestone, which imparts a rosy hue at sunset. But passengers alighting here need a good pair of walking shoes since the town is a mile and a half away, and half a mile lower, meaning a daunting climb from the village to the station. The Midland's engineers were far more interested in sweeping their long-distance passengers smoothly on to Scotland than bothering with the local communities along the way, and very few of the stations are close to the communities they purport to serve.

Soon we are at Ais Gill summit, marked by a large maroon sign, the highest point on the line at 1,169 feet above sea level and 1,000 feet higher than Leeds or Carlisle. The train has been climbing for forty-nine miles and in steam days it was a welcome chance for the firemen to mop their brows and ease off the shovel. But the climb was partly the cause of one of the most horrific accidents in British railway history. On an autumn day in 1913 two loaded passenger trains set off from Carlisle just eleven minutes apart. Both had difficulty raising steam because of a poor batch of coal, and the first train lost power and came to a halt. The driver of the second had climbed out onto the running board of the locomotive to refill the oil boxes, while the fireman struggled to inject more water into the boiler. Both failed to notice the signals at red and the locomotive slammed into the rear of the first train, killing fourteen and injuring thirty-eight. But there was also a less tragic outcome, since the accident led to the more widespread use of the Automatic Warning System, which long since has been a standard way of automatically applying the brakes when a signal is passed at danger. A memorial to the dead, newly restored by the Friends of the Settle and Carlisle Line, can be found in Kirkby Stephen cemetery.

People say there has long been a pall over this area, known as Mallerstang Common. In the eleventh century, the border warfare was so murderous and destructive that William the Conqueror's men were afraid to survey the area. Legend has it too that England's last wild boar was killed on the common. Nearby are the remains of Pendragon Castle, built by Uther Pendragon, who died after drinking the deliberately poisoned waters of a nearby spring. Sir Hugh Morville, one of the murderers of Thomas à Becket, also lived here, adding to the area's dark history.

There is a happier story at the next station, Garsdale, which once had water troughs for the express train steam engines to refill their tenders on the move after wheezing up the gradients. The troughs were the highest in England and were steam heated to stop them freezing over. Garsdale is most famous these days for its little statue of Ruswarp, the collie dog who attained fame by putting its paw print on the petition that helped to save the line in the 1980s. Ruswarp (pronounced Russup) belonged to Graham Nuttall from Burnley, the first secretary of the Friends of the Settle and Carlisle. In 1990 Nuttall went missing while walking in mid-Wales. When his body was found eleven weeks later, the dog was still by his master's side and lived just long enough to attend his funeral. Now Ruswarp is up there in the Settle and Carlisle Hall of Fame.

At Dent I am the only passenger to alight. I'm here in the darkness by chance because of a man I met on a train. It was on a journey to Edinburgh six months previously that I had struck up a conversation with Robin Hughes, a surveyor from Guildford, who had bought the old station buildings there and was busy restoring them. 'It used to be the second-highest in Britain until Princetown station on Dartmoor closed in 1956. Now it's in the record books. Come and try it out,' he said. 'I've just done up one of the snow huts. I'd be interested to know what you think.'

But as sharp Pennine gusts and horizontal rain streak across Widdale Fell, I start to wonder if I've been rash. As the lights of the last train south to Leeds vanish into the night, I wonder if I have arrived in a place that might make Cold Comfort Farm seem welcoming. A tattered notice by the platform gate proclaims, 'Dent station is very isolated. The village of Dent is more than four and a half miles away. Very occasionally, people find themselves stranded here. The house near the road is occupied by Roy and Jenny Holmes, who will help you.' The snow huts at the end of the old goods yard look dark and shuttered, and there doesn't look like any sign of life in the Holmeses' house. Will the key be under the mat as promised? (Robin Hughes is unavoidably in Surrey, he has told me.) I begin to contemplate a very cold night on the stone flags of the spartan platform shelter.

But, hurrah, the key is there, and after a couple of rusty-sounding twists it works. The snow huts, built in 1885, were once primitive billets for gangs stationed there through the winter for the back-breaking job of shovelling away the snow when it drifted onto the track. On the embankment above, silhouetted like stumps of rotten teeth, are lines of old railway sleepers, placed there to hold back drifting snow in the days before global warming, when Britain had proper winters. Fortunately, the only shovelling I have to do is to get the coal into the modern stove and light the newspaper and sticks. I wonder how the old gangers might have reacted if they had known that their damp little billet would one day be equipped with HD television, with halogen cooking and a wet room with underfloor heating. The only thing I have in common with the past is the fact that Dent is famous for having no mobile phone signal, and thus I am out of communication with the world.

Not entirely out of contact, however, since the legendary Mr and Mrs Holmes appear and offer me a lift into Dent village – 'Just wondering if you'd had anything to eat, love.' Roy, now retired, was the local electrician and bought the handsome gabled stationmaster's house back in the 1970s. It sits high on the brow of a hill (because Settle and Carlisle stationmasters of olden times were too grand to live near the platform). Because of its exposed position, it was one of the first houses in Britain to be fitted with double glazing. It is also graced by a magnificent fireplace made of the local blue limestone, known as Dent marble, which was also used to create the trimmings of Manchester Town Hall. Sleep in my snow hut is blissful, though insomniacs may be rattled from their beds by heavy coal and gypsum trains in the middle of the night.

Next morning the weather is grim, and the grey sky is still unleashing bucketloads. I take the train south, although it doesn't run until 10.07 – no commuting to work from here. There is more high opera as we enter the sinister portals of Blea Moor Tunnel, at 2,629 yards the longest on the line. 'A damp, terrible tunnel,' one historian called it. 'A horrible place . . . that drove men mad so they could go underground no more.' Another wrote, 'It was a devil to build, a devil to drive through on the foot-plate, for the enginemen always seemed glad to be out of it. A long dead dank smell of ageless rock and stale engine smoke greets the trains. Windows are hurriedly shut tight, while for two minutes, the vapours somehow find their way into the carriage.' Even today, engineers have to penetrate the blackness before the first train of the day to chip off the sooty black icicles which form inside the tunnel on winter nights.

We emerge from the gloom onto the treeless Blea Moor itself, whose very name reeks of desolation, and which might as well still be in the Ice Age, dotted as it is with drumlins – ancient piles of stones untouched for aeons since the glaciers met here. The train slows for the mighty Ribblehead Viaduct, now secured with concrete injected inside the piles. But only one train is allowed over at a time – just in case. On the ground more than a hundred feet below nothing grows and very little lives, although some enginemen claim to have seen wild cats – descendants of the creatures of the navvy camps and shanties that grew up here during the building of the line. Two thousand men lived here in primitive and squalid conditions during the five years it took to build the viaduct. The camps had names such as Sebastopol, Jordan and Jericho, derived from biblical locations and battles of the Crimean War. There were scenes of wild carousing and bloody drunken battles as the navvies struck terror into the local people. Records show that, in true Mayor of Casterbridge style, one man was prosecuted for selling his wife for a barrel of beer. Many died, not just from accidents but also from smallpox and other diseases. Now nothing is left of the camps except traces of the roadways where their huts once stood, though some say – as the evening mists swirl down the slopes from Whernside – that ghostly laughter can sometimes be heard echoing under the viaduct.

I get off at Ribblehead station in search of more tangible evidence of their memory. There's a little visitors' centre on the platform here, but this morning it's closed. Over my shoulder, as the rain turns to sleet, I can just glimpse the dirty grey hilltop of Whernside, whose 2,416-foot bulk dominates the Eden valley below. To the north, the sleet billows along the River Greta and over the arches of the magnificent Ribblehead Viaduct to grit-blast my cheeks.

There's a ballad, which I once heard at a folk club, which runs

And when the winter came it froze them to the floor.
It blew them off the viaduct and it killed them on Blea Moor.
Some died of the smallpox and some of cholera;
Chapal and St Leonards have many buried there.

And so I am crunching along a track to the little church of St Leonards, Chapel-en-le-Dale, in search of memories. My toes are frozen after the thirty-minute trek, but here is the little grey-slated church cloistered among the trees. And, sure enough, inside is the memorial, partly paid for by the guilty men of the Midland Railway itself. Was it enough to compensate for such human sacrifice in the cause of a commercial enterprise? Mr Allport and the members of the Midland board clearly thought it was.

> TO THE MEMORY OF THOSE WHO THROUGH ACCIDENTS LOST THEIR LIVES, IN CONSTRUCT-ING THE RAILWAY WORKS, BETWEEN SETTLE, AND DENT HEAD. THIS TABLET WAS ERECTED AT THE JOINT EXPENSE, OF THEIR FELLOW WORK-MEN AND THE MIDLAND RAILWAY COMPANY 1869 TO 1876

Darkness is gently falling as I get back in the train, which rattles down the gradients towards kinder country and eventually civilisation. But there are still sights, though less dramatic, to be seen, including the magnificent wrought-iron canopy at Hellifield station, the longest of its kind in Britain. Delicately set in the spandrels, heraldic wyverns, symbol of the Midland Railway, stand guard over the deserted platforms of this once-busy junction. Settle station, gateway to the Dales, by contrast is packed, and the train is suddenly filled with rucksacks, sweat and hiking boots. We have now left the Ribble Valley, and the train follows the River Aire all the way to Leeds, past Ilkley Moor, stopping briefly at Keighley, junction for the Keighley and Worth Valley preserved line, which in the summer dispatches tourist hordes to Haworth (alight here for the Brontë parsonage). It was on this little railway that Jenny Agutter once waved the red flag in that iconic film *The Railway Children*. Now we are sandwiched between electric commuter trains as we run into the Leeds/Bradford suburbs past the restored mohair and alpaca mills of Titus Salt's model working-class community of Saltaire, now home to the aspirational young middle classes of West Yorkshire.

Arrival in Leeds could not be more of an anticlimax. In few places in the world is such a heroic journey concluded in such modest style. The driver switches off the engine, slings his bag over his shoulder and vanishes into the crowd of home-going commuters. Even as recently as the 1960s our train would have been striding ahead on its next leg to St Pancras. Maybe it would have been a famous named express like the Thames–Clyde Express or the Waverley. Quite likely it would have had a sturdy Royal Scot Class steam loco, all brass and Brunswick-green paint, proudly on the front. (No. 46117, *Welsh Guardsman,* from Leeds Holbeck shed, was a favourite on this run.) White-coated stewards would be turning up the lamps and setting out starched tablecloths and silverware for dinner. A glass of champagne would be in prospect, as the aroma of *sole bonne femme* and beef Wellington wafted down from the kitchen car.

Could it happen again? Only in dreams. But the tough folk of the Friends of the Settle and Carlisle believe that their cherished railway will once again host Anglo-Scottish expresses that will speed all the way between London and Glasgow. They got it right once in the battle with British Rail bureaucrats that halted the closure of the line. And who is to say they are wrong now?

Watching the trains go by: Elderly 'Class 02' tank engine No. 31 Chale
moves an empty stock train out of Ryde St John's Road as the end of
steam on the Isle of Wight draws near in 1963.

CHAPTER THREE

THE 10.53 FROM RYDE — THE TUBE TRAIN THAT WENT TO THE SEASIDE

*Ryde Pier Head to Shanklin and Wootton,
via Smallbrook Junction*

Here is a riddle. I'm on a Tube train. I'm certain it's a Tube because it's painted in that comforting red which has been the uniform of London Transport since time began. The motors have that familiar whine and it smells reassuringly of the usual cocktail of dust and grease. As it rattles along, the driver poops that *poop* that is characteristic of all Tube trains and the sliding doors shut with the usual *ker-thud*. Yet there's something wrong here. Very wrong. (Although, curiously, it doesn't seem to bother my fellow passengers.) As we rattle along the track, there are views of an ultramarine sea and yachts with billowing sails, and little thatched cottages are strung along the shoreline. Pigs and cows are dotted around the fields. And so far we have only encountered one short tunnel. Hold on. Where are we? Is this some jaded city worker's Monday-morning dream? No, we're in the time warp that is the Isle of Wight.

Ever since the railway building mania of the 1840s, the Isle of Wight, just three miles across Spithead from Portsmouth, has been home to one of the most surreal and eccentric railway operations anywhere in the world. Given its mostly rural aspect and tiny population of 132,000, it is astonishing that the Isle of Wight ever had any railways at all, yet until the 1950s there were fifty-two miles of branch lines covering the entire island. In the 1960s the islanders not only fought Beeching's plans to close down all but one and a half miles of track, but actually succeeded in getting one of

the busiest sections electrified and retaining parts of the two exist-
ing branches as other seaside communities in the south of England,
such as Swanage and Lyme Regis, lost their trains altogether.

So my 10.53 to Shanklin service, sitting in the platform in Ryde
Pier Head station, has many reasons to feel proud of itself, its red
livery looking especially splendid on this sunny morning. Formed
of two former Tube cars which spent most of their lives carrying
weary Northern Line commuters from the West End and the City
to the northern and southern suburbs of High Barnet, Edgware
and Morden, the train and its sisters are the oldest in regular
service on the national rail network, built more than seventy years
ago. (I know this because the provenance is embossed in metal
plates below each door: 'Built by Metropolitan-Cammell Carriage
and Wagon Co. Ltd, Saltley, 1938'.)

But this is no heritage train, and there is no gracious retirement
by the seaside for this little Class 483 unit. The Island Line stations
are as much part of the national network as Waterloo or Clapham
Junction, and the services are run by the South West Trains
franchise, whose hard-headed boss Brian Souter is not famous for
nostalgia. 'Do you know that we're the most efficient railway in
Britain?' the guard tells me as he sells me an Island Liner ticket for
my eight-and-a-half-mile journey to the end of the line at
Shanklin. 'And these old girls run like a dream.' He reads from a
piece of paper with the official performance statistics for the past
four weeks: 'Punctuality 99.4 per cent. Reliability 100 per cent.
You can't argue with that, can you?'

Back in the pre-Benidorm, pre-Ford Anglia era of the 1950s, the
platforms here would be thronged with hundreds of thousands of
families dressed in their holiday best, arriving on the railway
company paddle steamers from Portsmouth. There was once a
glorious dome-roofed ballroom here, where if you were lucky you
might hear the latest hits of Victor Sylvester before going home to
your B & B in Seaview (H & C running water, interior-sprung
mattresses in every room). Today's foot passengers zip over on fast

Australian-owned catamarans, and most of the people who still choose the Isle of Wight over Faliraki or Phuket arrive on the car ferries that dock along the coast at Fishbourne. Today, the day after a bank holiday, Ryde Pier Head station has a rather melancholy air. There are fifteen minutes before the train goes, and I buy a Minghella ice cream ('famous in Ryde since 1950' but more famous still for being made by the parents of the late Oscar-winning film director Anthony Minghella) and chat to two boys fishing over the edge of one of the platforms next to a notice saying DO NOT FISH HERE. Nobody seems to care. 'We got four wrasse and a bream today – really nice ones.' The train is busy enough, with mothers and pushchairs, business types with sharp haircuts and suits over from Portsmouth and elderly couples tugging suitcases on wheels, taking the traditional route for a late-season holiday, perhaps to a 'nice guest house' in Shanklin or Ventnor. Sadly, there are no longer any porters, and the stand telling passengers to insert a coin for a luggage trolley is rusting and empty, the trolleys probably having been tipped into the ocean long ago.

But now it's time to MIND THE DOORS, and the train heads down the half-mile length of the pier as purposefully as it must have accelerated out of East Finchley for Charing Cross, past the rusting remains of the diesel tramway, with its own separate tracks, which functioned until 1969. In fact rust and genteel decline have defined the entire transport history of the island, which has always been a kind of anachronism, operating with the equipment of at least the previous generation. In the nineteenth century there were three different companies, with names like the Freshwater, Yarmouth and Newport Railway, running a ragbag of ancient locomotives over single-track branch lines which mostly seemed to go to nowhere. Between the wars the railways still captured the flavour of the 1890s, when Queen Victoria was in residence at her favourite home, Osborne House, near Cowes. And from the 1950s until the end of steam in 1966 the railway was a perfectly preserved museum of the pre-grouping world before 1923, despite the modern liveries. Little tank engines pottered round single-track secondary routes tugging wooden-panelled non-corridor coaches. And now the Tube trains, which made their first outing when Neville Chamberlain was prime minister, are the biggest anachronism of them all.

There are many who say that the Isle of Wight never recovered from the death of Queen Victoria, when the smart set – who built their holiday homes to be close to Her Majesty and possibly get invited round for a fairy cake and some iced tea with Tennyson and Dickens – packed up and went home. But it has had moments of modernity since then. Parked on the sand next to Ryde Esplanade station is the Hovertravel hovercraft, waiting for its next flight to Southsea. As every schoolboy reader of the *Eagle* knows, this was a Great British Invention of the 1950s developed in the Isle of Wight by Saunders-Roe at Cowes. But sadly, like many other Great British Inventions, including flying boats, also built by Saunders-Roe but in the 1930s, hovercraft are no longer so futuristic. Passenger services have fallen out of favour and the Ryde–Southsea service is the last remaining in Britain. 'Typical,' people say. The Isle of Wight can't resist clinging on to its past.

Even the station name Esplanade – the only one in Britain – is redolent of Ryde's Victorian heyday (there was once a Promenade station in Morecambe, but this closed in 1994). Esplanades, by definition, are not modern things, and reek of an idealised past – sandcastles, buckets and spades, the Punch and Judy man and donkey rides. Holidays and nostalgia are always a heady mix, and recollections of childhood summers in south coast holiday resorts are often so frozen in time as to exclude the modern reality of poverty, decline and unemployment which blights so many of them. Even so, Ryde appears rather perky and vibrant this morning, with the little shops of Union Street looking much as they might have done in the days when Oscar Wilde and Karl Marx might have strolled past during their stays on the island. In the Royal Esplanade Hotel on the seafront, Josef, the waiter who serves me morning coffee, is in jovial mood telling me about the 'motor scooter festival' that took place the previous day – the world's biggest. Back in the 1960s the Vespa crowd used to go to Margate for a punch-up; now middle-aged and more respectable, they come to Ryde for tea and cakes. 'Such nice people,' Josef tells me. 'No trouble. No trouble at all.' A toot on the whistle as the next train south arrives at Esplanade station over the road. It's all perfectly in period. In its post-war heyday our Tube train would almost certainly have carried passengers to Leicester Square to watch Gregory Peck and Audrey Hepburn – riding side saddle – on their Vespa buzzing through the streets of Rome in *Roman Holiday*.

But now we're heading through the 391-yard tunnel to Ryde St John's Road. We must be thankful for the tunnel. Its small diameter is partly responsible for the railway becoming a kind of working museum, since it's always been difficult to find trains to fit the line. It also explains why the Tubes were such a godsend. Their arrival allowed engineers to raise the floor of the tunnel so that it would flood less frequently at high tide, although there is still an operative pumping station near the Esplanade.

Lucky old Ryde. It is one of the smallest towns in Britain to have three stations of its own, and St John's Road is the nerve centre of the railway – the Crewe, the Doncaster and the Swindon of the island, rolled into one. Literally, since almost all Britain's great Victorian railway works of the past have been closed or sold off, and Jess Harper and his engineering team at Ryde – the works building still bearing the insignia of the old Southern Railway – are the last on the national network still maintaining their own rolling stock. And they reckon they know more about old Tube trains than even the people at London Underground; after all, they have been keeping them going for forty-five years.

Back in 1963, when Beeching proposed closure of the entire Isle of Wight network except for the section between the Esplanade and the ferry terminal at the end of Ryde pier, he was mainly influenced by the fact that the rolling stock on the island was ancient and would have to be replaced. The carriages dated from before the First World War, cast-offs from the London, Brighton and South Coast and London, Chatham and Dover railways. The little Victorian O2 Class 0-4-4 tanks were already hand-me-downs from Waterloo suburban services when they were transferred from the mainland by the Southern Railway in 1922. Although the little engines ran what in 1966 was the most intensive single-track service in Britain, hauling holiday trains up to ten coaches long, they were literally worn out, with cracked frames and wonky bogies, and the pumps that operated the Westinghouse brakes had to be encased in metal sheets to stop them spitting scalding water on unwary passengers. The Isle of Wight lines might have been a paradise for transport enthusiasts, who flocked there from all over the country, but there was a simple answer for Beeching as to what to do with all these geriatric trains – eliminate them.

But Beeching didn't get his way entirely, and it was announced in 1964 that the busiest part of the line, from Ryde to Shanklin, was to be saved. Miraculously, the old Southern Region decided to electrify it and bought a job lot of redundant London Tube stock from the 1920s at a cost of between £120 and £200 a carriage. These elderly trains, of a design which ran over the Piccadilly, Central and Bakerloo Lines and ended their London lives on the old Northern City Line from Moorgate to Finsbury Park, were not much younger than the trains they were replacing, and it is instructive that as the first cars were being sent to the Isle of Wight one of their sister coaches went on display at the Science Museum in London. These early Tubes have now gone to the scrapyard, being replaced by 'young things' from 1938, which have operated the Ryde line since.

Ryde St John's Road is a cheery place where many of the old Victorian buildings survive and the cast-iron spandrels supporting the canopies bear the monogram of the original Isle of Wight Railway, opened in 1864. There is a handsome Victorian signal box, which controls the whole line, festooned with tubs of flowers. On the up platform is one of the most prolific displays of colour-coordinated flowers I have ever seen on a railway station – I have to touch the giant red lilies, begonias and busy lizzies to make sure they are not made of plastic. The displays are done by local disabled people, Tony Dickinson, the station manager, tells me. Tony, a slick young man with a neat white shirt and tie, with a South West Trains badge on a clip, controls all the stations on the lines, and his office is a buzzy place shared with drivers and conductors drinking from steaming mugs of tea. 'We've had a good year,' he tells me. 'A total of 1.3 million passengers – I'm very pleased.' Not surprising, since this means that nearly half the 2.7 million passengers who travel to the Isle of Wight each year get aboard one of his Tube trains. Not exactly Piccadilly Circus, but not bad for a small island off the Hampshire coast. 'And we're operating sixty-seven trains a day,' he tells me. I am too polite to remind him that recent economies mean the service runs to an odd timetable, with alternating intervals of twenty and forty minutes between trains. Not exactly convenient for most people.

All traces of the engine sheds, which were once outside his office and in the 1960s attracted droves of young boys who preferred the thrill of trainspotting to a boring afternoon on the beach with their parents, have gone. However such is the measure of affection still held for the little locos running at the end of steam that their handsome brass nameplates (all commemorating island towns and villages) can fetch up to £15,000 at auctions of railwayana.

But time to head off on the next train south to the island's newest station, Smallbrook Junction, one of a tiny number of stations in British railway history never to have had any external access. This is where the lines to Newport, the island's capital, and Cowes once diverged, until Beeching got his hands on them. A signal box once stood here and the signalman doled out tokens allowing track access to the respective drivers as they raced off with their trains full of holidaymakers down the lines to Ventnor (then the terminus of the Shanklin line) and to Cowes. In the 1960s it was the busiest mechanical junction box in southern England. But the Cowes line was too good to lose and a bunch of preservation-ists saved part of it to become what is now the Isle of Wight Steam Railway. In an astonishing act of generosity, the old British Rail management built Smallbrook Junction station in 1991 to allow passengers to change from the Tube trains on the Shanklin line.

But renewals since have been rare – and the platform and signal box at Brading, the next station down the line, are now weed-grown and derelict, with the boarded-up station setting the tone for the rest of the line. At Sandown, the loveliest resort on the island with wide sandy beaches, the station cafe is derelict, with dust-covered tables visible through a broken window, although the newspaper kiosk is still open, bearing its former WH Smith sign, proclaiming in faded paint, NEWSPAPERS AND MAGAZINES POSTED ANYWHERE IN THE COUNTRY. A notice on the toilets announces that they close each day at 12.25 p.m. – a time at which bladders presumably cease to function and which explains why, at the Shanklin terminus, a man is hosing down the subway with a water-ing can of disinfectant. Wasn't like this once. I have a black and white photograph of Shanklin from 1963, spruce and smart, with hundreds of folk in their holiday best making their way to the taxi rank for their seafront hotels. There is not a single taxi here today and the walk down to the beach is a long one, although some of the best sands in the south of England make it worth the effort.

Until 1966 the trains went on from here to Ventnor, through a 1,312-yard tunnel under St Boniface Down to a spectacular station set in a chalk cutting. But the tunnel, which is now used by the local water authority, would be far too expensive to reopen. It is tempting to walk the rest of the course of the line over the down, but I must return to Ryde because I have an appointment with a monk. Not to confess uncharitable thoughts about the rather run-down state of the railway, for whose continued existence we must be grateful, but because I am to stay tonight with a community of Benedictine monks at the Grade I-listed Quarr Abbey near Fishbourne.

I, like many other travellers to the Isle of Wight, have long held eternally sunny images of the island imprinted on my mind after being taken on holiday there by my parents as a child, and one of these was of Quarr, its pink bricks glowing in a kind of perpetual sunset. Would it still be there? I sent an email, not expecting a reply, but within a day a message had pinged back – from Father Nicholas Spencer, the guestmaster, who told me how interested he was in the Isle of Wight railways and that I could come and stay the night at the abbey if I liked. There's long been a 'general kinship between the religious life and the railway scene', as Canon Roger Lloyd put it in his book *The Fascination of Railways*. Archbishop of Canterbury William Temple is said to have memorised the railway timetable of his day; Canon Victor Whitechurch of Christ Church Oxford was the creator of the vegetarian railway detective Thorpe Hazell, and the Reverend Wilbert Awdry was, of course, the author of the Thomas the Tank Engine books. Fans of the Ealing comedy *The Titfield Thunderbolt* will recall that the train was driven by the local vicar.

So, as darkness falls, I am on the No. 9 bus along the Newport Road, asking the driver to put me off at the abbey. 'Never been there myself,' he says. 'I expect you'll find some spooky type answering the door. If you need to escape, we're running until midnight.' Actually there appears to be nobody around at all when I ring the bell, and after twisting the handles on the various great oak doors of the monastery and the church, I find one that creaks open into a lobby. Here too the doors are locked, but under a heavy metal bolt is a scrawled note telling me to wait. I sit in the deserted quadrangle under the cypresses as the dusk settles for seemingly ages. A pair of red squirrels play around my feet. Might I have to head back to the bus stop after all? Then a slight figure, black habit flapping, comes running out of the church. 'So sorry to keep you.' This is the decidedly un-spooky Father Spencer, who has been at a meeting. 'There are only nine of us,' he tells me, 'in a monastery that was designed for 120. I take it you are coming to dinner? Don't forget that we eat in total silence.' He shows me into a vast refectory with long polished oak tables in semi-darkness. The monks sit at one end of the room and a table is set for me at the other. 'But first you must shake hands with the abbot – who is a large red-faced Irishman with silver hair. When you have finished eating, you can get up and leave.' The food is surprisingly good – a meat and lentil pie with red kidney beans and fragrant apples from the monastery garden – which is reflected in the speed with which the monks eat. There is a rapid scraping of cutlery on plates, and soon everyone is heading for the exit.

Afterwards, Father Nicholas shows me round the vast abbey church of Our Lady of Quarr, built in 1912 by the French monk-architect Dom Paul Bellot, who brought a community of monks from Solesmes in France, driven out by the anti-clericalism of the time. Constructed of Belgian brick by local workmen who had never put up anything bigger than a house, it is like nothing else to be found in Britain. Pevsner calls it 'brilliant' and a work of inter-national importance, comparing it with the achievement of the Catalan architect Gaudi. But I notice it is falling apart in places, with cracks in the brickwork over the nave, missing pointing and leaking gutters. 'It's hard work for such a few of us to keep it going,' says Father Nicholas, a blunt but charming man who comes from Millom in Cumbria, and whose father was the manager of Barrow steelworks. 'I've been here twenty-six years and I always wanted to be a monk and I've never doubted that I did the right thing. But our community is a small one. The youngest is forty-five and the oldest over ninety. The one thing I pray for above all is that it will be enlarged. We have a few possibilities . . .' He looks doubtful. And what about the Isle of Wight Steam Railway? 'I've never been on it, although I would like to have done so. You see, I have never had enough money for the fare.'

As well as looking after guests, Father Nicholas is the abbey bee-keeper and runs a bookbindery in the basement. He shows me a magnificent copy of Oscar Wilde's *Ballad of Reading Gaol*, ornamented with a gallows with the rope represented in relief in braided leather. Appropriate fare for a community of monks? I don't know. 'But do come to compline.' This is a night service, one of the five acts of worship held in the church every day of the year, starting at 5 a.m. I wonder how the monks find the time to do all the mundane jobs necessary to keep the monastery running. Walking to the darkened church with the moon reflected on the slate roof and listening to the same Gregorian chant that has been sung for more than 1,500 years is a humbling experience. The rule of St Benedict states that every monastery guest should be 'received as Christ'. I think that the monks haven't failed in their duty when Father Nicholas waves me off to the bus stop in the morning.

It is ironic that the Southern Vectis Omnibus Company – the monopoly bus service provider on the island – was founded by the Southern Railway back in 1929, as it was instrumental in killing off large parts of the railway in the 1960s. You can see why as I get off the bus at Wootton, the terminus of the preserved Isle of Wight Steam Railway, which once ran all the way from Ryde to Newport and Cowes. The modern two-tone green buses run every nine minutes and carry slogans such as THE SLEEK WAY TO TRAVEL. COOL OR WHAT? 'Cool' is a term that could never be applied to the railways of the Isle of Wight and it's no wonder the Cowes line was seen off by the buses. But enough of the line remains to catch a train back along the five and a half miles to Smallbrook Junction. I buy a ticket from a man in a baggy uniform with a remarkable resemblance to Charles Hawtrey, and in the platform a little former War Department saddle-tank locomotive is fussing around its train – the familiar *blink-blonk-hiss* of the Westinghouse brake pump gives the impression that it is impatient to leave.

The Isle of Wight Steam Railway is almost unique among heritage lines in that the volunteers who run it got their act together almost immediately after closure and have a vast collection of authentic Victorian rolling stock. 'Why then the relatively modern steam loco?' I ask Charles Hawtrey. 'Well, she's reliable for a start,' he tells me. 'And our star loco, *Calbourne*, is in the works having her boiler done.' No. 24 *Calbourne* was one of the last locos to work on the line before British Rail closed it. He tells me a story about how the volunteers acquired it. 'The wildlife artist David

Shepherd wanted to save a steam loco from the scrapyard, so he went to the office of Ian Allan, the trainspotters' book publisher, to ask for advice. The publisher told him, "David, if you've got £500 to spend, why don't you buy an 02 tank engine". And do you know, she's been running for us twice as long as she ran for BR!'

The train jogs along through a silver birch wood, the leaves just tinged with autumn red. It's the perfect period-piece slow train straight out of Philip Larkin's *Whitsun Weddings*: a warm afternoon, 'all windows down, all cushions hot', ambling along with 'shuffling gouts of steam'. The advertisements under the luggage racks offer Holiday Runabout Tickets for summer 1950 at a modest ten and sixpence, first class for fifteen shillings. Or how about 'Southern Railway restaurant cars on principal trains. Lunch, two and sixpence, dinner, three and sixpence. Tea and light refreshments at modest prices.' At the Southern's Charing Cross Hotel there are 'gas fires and telephones in every room'. But we're back to the real world at Havenstreet, the headquarters of the line – once a modest single-track platform with a siding serving a gasworks, now with its gift shop, tearoom and museum, the nerve centre of one of the island's most popular tourist attractions.

It's presided over with schoolmasterly precision by Alan Doe, the operations manager, a retired headmaster from Cornwall in charge of nineteen paid staff and 200 volunteers 'Why are we so special?' He breaks off to order two tins of Brasso over the phone. 'It's because we have original locomotives and original stations, with original carriages running on lines they used to work on. We're a proper working heritage site.' Now there's a gleam in his eye. 'Let me show you this.' He leads me across the tracks to a shed away from the public gaze. Inside are two relatively modern but rusty 1940s Ivatt Class 2-6-2 tank locomotives once earmarked by British Railways to work the line when the Victorian tank engines went. It never happened because the Tube trains were drafted in. 'Some old gents bought these at the end of steam, but they've got past the point of restoring them so they've given them to us. And soon we're going to get them running.' A secret cache of steam engines that haven't run for nearly half a century? It's every rail enthusiast's fantasy and Alan Doe's equivalent of the back catalogue of his thriving steam railway.

But what future for the electrified Island Line, with its super-annuated Tubes? Can it survive in the bean-counting world of the modern railway? Until recently the line received the biggest subsidy per passenger of any in Britain. To get the answer, everyone says, 'You'll have to ask Bobby.' Bobby Lock is the island's rail development officer, who, according to local legend, is responsible single-handedly for transforming the line's fortunes – a one-woman publicity machine and consciousness-raiser. Even gritty old railwaymen defer to her. John Little, South West Trains' operating manager, says of her efforts: 'Now the railway has soul.' I track Bobby down to her home in Cowes, on the way attempting to decipher the remains of the old station. But there is nothing to be seen – it has disappeared without trace under a Co-op supermarket. But Bobby, small and blonde and busy feeding tea to her three-year-old daughter, is in upbeat mood. She shows me some safety posters that have been designed for the railway by local schoolchildren. 'Of course the line won't close. Not now. We all love it too much. And I hear London Underground have a nice batch of Tube trains soon to be retired from the Victoria Line …' I get the sense the Tube bosses in London won't be in a position to refuse her.

Next morning, when I head back for Portsmouth, the pickets are out at Ryde bus station. It turns out there's a one-day bus strike on the island. And with high autumn winds whipping the Solent to a froth, none of the sleek catamaran ferries to the mainland are running because of the weather. But Bobby's Tube trains are still doughtily shuttling up and down the line to Shanklin. And eventually, after an hour's wait, an old-style 'vomit bucket' ferry turns up at the pier head. 'It may be a bit rolly and unpleasant,' announces the captain over the intercom, 'but we'll make it to the other side eventually.' Old trains, old ferries. But at least they get you there.

London's last terminus: Great Western Railway 'Hall Class'
No. 6990 Witherslack Hall at Marylebone in June 1948. This was
once the sleepiest of stations where the atmosphere was described
as one of 'cloistered calm'.

CHAPTER FOUR

THE 10.30 FROM WREXHAM CENTRAL – UP THE LINE TO LONDON'S LAST TERMINUS

Wrexham Central to London Marylebone,
via Gobowen, Shrewsbury, Wolverhampton, Banbury
and High Wycombe

'Go through the multi-storey,' says the nice young man in the Games Workshop. 'Take a left and you'll see a pile of Asda catalogues.' I'm in a bleak shopping centre in Wrexham, North Wales, looking for what must be the most forlorn railway terminus in Britain. And here it is, tucked in between Argos Extra and Asda Living. It may have a grand-sounding name, but Wrexham Central is nothing more than a single track and a large red set of buffers sand-wiched between the shops. There are piles of broken glass on the platform and a group of youths flick stones at beer cans on the track.

It is a small miracle that this, the farthest outpost of one of the grandest railway companies in the land, which once spread its tentacles from Scarborough to Stratford-upon-Avon and from Newcastle to Neath, should have survived in this inhospitable place. Once you could book a ticket at London's Marylebone station and travel behind the magnificent green engines of the Great Central Railway, pompously named after the directors of the board, on the line to Wrexham (or Manchester or Sheffield, Nottingham or Hull) without leaving the company's metals.

It is hard to imagine on this rainy morning in Wrexham that this was part of one of the most grandly conceived projects of the Railway Age. Back in the 1890s, Sir Edward Watkin, chairman of the Manchester, Sheffield and Lincolnshire, as the Great Central was then known, had a dream. It wasn't enough to fill the company's coffers with the profits from humping coal and iron across the Pennines; he would build a new line to London. Never mind that all the other railway companies had already built their own lines to the capital, he would park his own terminus in the Euston Road to rival Euston, St Pancras and King's Cross. But Sir Edward, described by one of his contemporaries as a 'gambler and a megalomaniac', wasn't going to stop there. There was an even grander master plan. In 1881 he promoted a parliamentary bill to build the first Channel tunnel, even getting so far as to begin drilling a pilot tunnel into the chalk, where he audaciously hosted a champagne party for investors. Soon, he promised them, it would be possible to travel direct from the industrial towns of northern England to the Continent and beyond. The rewards would be beyond compare.

But it was all doomed. The magnificent engineering of Watkin's London extension rivalled that of Stephenson and Brunel, with a generous loading gauge, easy gradients and just one level crossing in its entire length. But despite the huge razzmatazz when it opened in 1899, with a splendid dinner hosted on the station platform, the last conventional main line to be built in Britain was simply too late and never caught on. It was the first main line to lose its passenger services, and fizzled out ignominiously at the hands of Beeching in 1966, when the once-grand expresses, such as the Master Cutler and South Yorkshireman, had dwindled to three semi-fast trains a day to Nottingham, pulled by filthy, wheezing Black Five Class steam locomotives. The Manchester, Sheffield and Lincolnshire, dubbed the 'Money Sunk and Lost', had spawned a new acronym in the Great Central, the Gone Completely. But not entirely, as we shall soon discover. Watkin was simply ahead of his time and would have enjoyed the irony that although it took Britain another century to get round to building its next new main line, this one really did run through a Channel tunnel.

Just imagine it. Book me a ticket from Wrexham to Vienna or St Petersburg. How about Istanbul? Vladivostock even? Yes, and I'd like a first-class sleeping berth too. 'Rapid Travel in Luxury' was the slogan. 'Jason fought for the Golden Fleece in mezzotint panels on the dining car ceilings,' observed the railway historian C Hamilton Ellis, 'and as you lounged on a splendiferous pew of carved oak and figured plush, the sun, shining through coloured glass deck lights, gave a deliciously bizarre quality to the complexion of the lady opposite.'

But hold on a minute. Here I am, the only passenger on a utilitarian little two-coach Class 150 diesel train, which has just growled across the Dee through the grimiest part of industrial North Wales along what is euphemistically known as the Borderlands Line. (Badlands might be more appropriate, I speculate.) 'Not many people get on here,' says the conductor. Which is just as well since nobody has bothered to change the destination blind since the train left the depot this morning – it still reads 'Crewe'. 'It's them up at the Welsh parliament that keeps us going. You can't shut a railway in Wales these days, y'know. Too much pride, boy.'

But in its own way this is the start of a very special journey indeed, for I am on my way from Wrexham to Marylebone, taking, improbably, one of the most luxurious train journeys in modern Britain, with the kind of service last seen in the heyday of the 1930s and almost entirely vanished from the corporate, privatised railway. And this starting from a town that not even the most optimistic would regard as one of the commercial hotspots of Wales, let alone the UK.

But first we must suffer the two-minute grind over weed-covered track and rattling curves to Wrexham General, the next stop down the line, where I spy something altogether far grander – a gleaming silver Class 67 express diesel loco revving its engines at the head of the 11.33 a.m. Wrexham and Shropshire Railway express to London Marylebone.

Nearly twenty years down the line, few would disagree that John Major's privatisation of the railways in 1994 was a botch. Instead of creating competition and choice for passengers, it simply replicated the monopoly of British Railways by carving up the turf between powerful private firms who bid for the franchises. At the beginning of that century you could have got a rival train from almost anywhere to anywhere – which is how the old Great Central put its tanks on the lawn of the Great Western by building its own station here in Wrexham. At that time there were three other rail companies that could deliver you here: you could take your pick from the Great Western, the Cambrian and the London and North Western companies. Now the barons of the rail franchise fiefdoms mostly rule their territory absolutely. Try travelling from London to Bristol or Manchester and asking the booking clerk, 'Can I have an alternative, please?' In Scotland and Wales the private companies exert total monopolies, if you exclude the trains that arrive from England.

Luckily, there was a small get-out in the privatisation laws, which is how I come to be settling back into the cushions of an armchair in this first class Mark III restaurant car – generally reckoned to be the most comfortable ever built on the railway – where I am already being offered a glass of chilled Pouilly-Fuissé. The reason Wrexham got lucky, compared with posh Chester a short ride up the tracks, was a clause called 'open access', which allowed the tiny Wrexham and Shropshire Railway to start the service. Who would have guessed that when BR killed off through trains from Wrexham to London in the 1960s that there would ever again be a service to London, let alone four trains a day, with a choice of operators (there is also a daily return trip to Euston, run by Virgin)? Yet the law allows anyone who can spot a gap in the market missed by the big firms to apply to the regulators to run their own competing trains. Hull and Sunderland – cities down on their luck like Wrexham – have also been put back on the main line map in this way.

The key to success for these small companies is quality of service. On my 11.23 to Marylebone, the approach is decidedly upmarket, with proper china and cutlery on the tables – a deliberate harking back to the days when trains were unhurried, the staff attentive and the styrofoam cup had not been invented. Unlike Wrexham Central, the General station is full of sleepy Edwardian charm, virtually unchanged since it was built in 'French pavilion' style by the Great Western Railway in 1912. You might imagine John

Betjeman enjoying a buttered Welsh cake in the tearoom here, where there are real flowers in vases on the tables. At the end of the platform an ivy-covered goods shed slumbers into dereliction. To add to the air of history, this is the last station in Britain to retain the title of 'General', once an epithet sported in many towns, including Cardiff and Reading. Most of the stations once entitled 'Victoria' or 'Halt' or 'Road' have now been consigned to the bin of the modern corporate railway, although a few survive. Even the train itself, though modern in concept, is a throwback to a less standardised age, when retired express engines would be relegated to secondary duties with a handful of elderly coaches which may have done service on the main line a long time ago, but are now deemed fit only to creak along secondary routes.

Our Class 67 locomotive, No. 67012, elegaically named *A Shropshire Lad*, is one of the most modern on the system – built in 2000 and designed to run at 125 mph. Yet it too is already an anachronism. Commissioned from Alsthom in Spain to speed fast mail trains across the system, the class was made redundant when the Post Office transferred the mail to the roads in 2004. There's not much use for the 67s these days. Two are dedicated to the royal train. Others trundle sleeping cars over the Highland lines in Scotland. But the rest potter round the system looking rather lost, without much else to do. There are only three carriages on the train, all still in the British Rail Inter-City grey and blue livery of the 1980s. Once they operated on crack Anglo-Scottish expresses from Euston. But, retired from front-line duty, these well-appointed coaches are modern antiques more highly regarded by many passengers than the Pendolino trains that replaced them, and are especially suited to their present, gentler task. Their expansive legroom, wide windows and – luxury of luxuries on the modern railway – seats that line up with the windows will do nicely to ease us on this May afternoon through some of the best of rural Britain – weaving across the border of England and Wales, through the heart of the Midlands, surmounting the Chilterns into Betjeman's Metroland, and on through the tunnel beneath

Lord's Cricket Ground into the red-brick and terracotta Marylebone station.

There is probably no line in Britain more evocative of the secondary railway of yesteryear than this one, heading south through the Welsh Marches, passing through rolling countryside with splendid castles and towns steeped in history. It has a special place in the hearts of railway enthusiasts since it was on the bottom leg of this line, from Hereford to Newport, that steam returned to the British Railways main line in 1971, three years after everyone thought it had gone for ever. The run, by the Great Western Railway's most famous locomotive *King George V*, heralded a revival of steam which culminated in 2009 with the completion of the *Tornado*, the first brand new steam express locomotive built in Britain since 1960.

Heading south from Wrexham, there are wooden signal boxes and traditional semaphore signalling, where signallers still pull wires on pulleys that raise or lower heavy pieces of machinery in a tradition that goes back to the very birth of the railway. This is a world of technology that has barely heard of the microchip, let alone the LED, yet is as safe, in its clunking mechanical way, as anything that has come since. The train picks up speed past the spoil tips that once defined this former coal and steel town, now overgrown with grass. There is evidence of its other heritage too. The hillside to the west was once home to twenty-four chapels and three churches, though these are now swamped by dreary modern housing estates. We pass through the remains of several little wayside stations, closed in the 1960s but with solid buildings refusing to die amid the undergrowth, and eventually pull up at Ruabon, whose Tudor-style stone station is sadly boarded up, leaving today's passengers to huddle in a miserable bus shelter on the platform. Here you could once change trains for Llangollen ('alight here for the Eisteddfod') and Barmouth on the coast – though luckily a stretch of this line survives as the Llangollen Railway, one of the most popular preserved lines in Wales.

Running through the remains of Cefn station, closed in 1960, even before Beeching, those with keen ears can hear a change in the note of the wheels on the track as the train rattles onto the Cefn–Mawr Viaduct. Built in 1848 of the local pale golden stone this spectacular structure has nineteen arches and is 147 feet high. The local landowners who opposed it so vigorously at the time of its building could hardly have imagined its mellow fit with the landscape today. Such was the level of local opposition that the Scottish designer Henry Robertson had to carry out his surveys by night, since objectors threatened to 'throw the man and his theodolite into the canal', according to reports at the time. But, as in so many cases with railways such as this, the engineering was done with supreme good taste, using good local materials. After all, who wouldn't want a bit of distinguished architecture at the end of your estate, built by the likes, in this case, of the most distinguished civil engineer of the day, Thomas Brassey? The truth was that the wealthy landowners who threw tantrums were merely after the best compensation terms. Afterwards, they sat in their country houses and enjoyed both the cash and the trains.

On the east side of the line there is the great loop of the River Dee; on the west the view is of Offa's Dyke, and a mile upstream you can see the famous Pontcysyllte aqueduct built by Thomas Telford to carry the Llangollen branch of the Shropshire Union Canal. Completed in 1805, it is the longest and highest aqueduct in Britain, a Grade I-listed building and a World Heritage Site. But don't muse on the idyll for too long because round the curve is an almighty slap in the face from the giant Krononspan MDF works, the third-largest in the world, a smoking and fuming vision of hell, spreading across a hundred acres amid mountains of wood pulp. But at least the logs for processing arrive in an ecologically sound way – by train from Eskdalemuir in Scotland.

Serenity is restored as we pass the magnificent medieval fortress of Chirk Castle in the woods to the west, the last Edward I castle still lived in today, and emerge from a cutting onto Chirk Viaduct. This is a breathtaking sight, the line soaring over the river Ceiriog and the border into England on sixteen arches of honey-coloured stone. On the east side, almost touching it but a little lower, runs the canal on the matching masonry of Telford's 1801 aqueduct. The water is contained in a vast iron trough, the plates for which were cast at nearby Ketley. This is a transport archaeologist's paradise, since below is the trackbed of the little narrow-gauge Glyn Valley Tramway, built to carry slate across the valley. It closed in 1935, but now a group of enthusiasts are hoping to reopen it. How do we know we are back in England? Because Gobowen station is the first on the route without dual language signs. GOBOWEN FOR OSWESTRY it announces grandly in large wooden letters on a huge black and white sign, unchanged since Great Western days. It is a prompt for me to get off, since waiting on the platform is the man who probably does more to promote the line than any other. 'Shall I put the kettle on?' he asks.

Martin Evans runs the ticket office here, although he is not employed by a railway company. He rents part of the station building, where he runs a private travel agency and also acts as booking clerk. Without him, Gobowen would be as cold and bleak as the other boarded-up and unstaffed stations along the line. Chairman of the Shrewsbury–Chester Rail Users Association, Martin is one of the army of people who fiercely guard the welfare of country railways across the land. Neither professional railwaymen nor train buffs, they believe passionately in the future of their local rail line. Any future Beeching should beware of people like Martin.

'It was terrible the way they cut the line back from the days when the Kings and Castles would steam in from Birkenhead with the London trains in the 1960s,' he tells me as we drink coffee from GWR-monogrammed cups in the snug waiting room, which must be one of the comfiest on the entire network, complete with a library of books for passengers to browse while they wait for their train. Things are looking up now, though. The Welsh Assembly has underwritten a through service from Cardiff to Holyhead, and now there's the Wrexham and Shropshire with its direct trains to London. 'Do you know, their guards use whistles? I don't think I've heard the sound of a train whistle for years!'

Martin's next ambition is to get Network Rail to double the single track between Wrexham to Chester, cut back as part of the Beeching economies. 'And see that branch down there,' he says, pointing to a rusting set of lines veering away from the bay platform? 'We might get that reopened too.' This was the route to Oswestry, headquarters of the old Cambrian Railway, mothballed by the Department for Transport after it closed in 1971. The company's magnificent Victorian locomotive works still survives in the town – the 'Swindon of Shropshire' as it was once known.

Before I head on to Shrewsbury to catch the next Wrexham and Shropshire train to London, Martin shows me round the station with its gorgeous Florentine building, complete with campanile, built of ashlar stone. It was recently restored with a grant from English Heritage and painted a gentle powder blue. The old GWR signs are actually replicas, Martin tells me, and one has been taken away for repainting. 'But, look, take some photographs,' he urges. 'There's a nice view of the signal box.' I don't mention the ugly uPVC windows that have been installed to replace the old wooden ones. There is nothing on Gobowen station of which he is not proud, including a little children's area made in the shape of an old railway carriage. He presses a book on the history of the line into my hand. 'Borrow it,' he says. 'No hurry about getting it back.' In Gobowen there's no hurry. No hurry at all.

I travel south to Shrewsbury on the next stopping train, where the passengers seem mostly to be shoppers and students. In the seat opposite me a young mother struggles with a fractious two-year-old. Chester to Shrewsbury is neither a branch line yet nor a main line either – unpretentious, going nowhere very fast – but lines like this in gentle rural surroundings remain the sinews of the national rail system. Their charm, wrote David St John Thomas in *The Country Railway* in 1976,

> was no one thing, any more than a superb landscape painting
> is any one of its ingredients. It was the total railway in the
> countryside, serving it as part of it, the smell of steam and
> oil, the people arriving and departing, the ticket racks in the

booking office from which you could tell how many people had gone where on the previous day – the tail of the signal-man's dog flopping on the lino, asking for attention.

If only it were still so. Many of the intermediate stations on this line have closed and their remains flash by – all with names straight out of Flanders and Swann: Whittington, Rednal and West Felton, Baschurch and Leaton. Only the ghosts of booking clerks or signalmen's dogs here. The arrival of the conductor flourishing his ticket machine as we pass through the remnants of Baschurch means I nearly miss one of the famous local landmarks – the hill to the north-east is thought to be Pengwern, seat of Prince Cynddylan, the seventh-century ruler of Powys.

Shrewsbury is perhaps the last major old-fashioned country junction left in Britain. From here lines meander gently through the most rural parts of Wales and the Borders. Until the arrival of the Wrexham and Shropshire in 2008 there had been no through services to London since Virgin abandoned them in 2001. Now the station is operated by Arriva Trains Wales, who have slapped their ugly turquoise house colours on every conceivable bit of paintwork, turning this grand old lady, designed by T M Penson in 1848 in the style of a miniature Houses of Parliament, into something of a tart. But the corporate image has failed to eradicate the charm. It's easy to imagine the young Darwin embarking here after his time at Shrewsbury School for his first journey up to Cambridge. Now the weeds grow through the tracks and pigeons flap under the canopies, defecating on the little stone heads carved into the roof bosses. Long-disused platform ends are a reminder of the days when grand trains of twelve carriages stopped here. Now six coaches comprise a very long train indeed.

As we approach from the north, passing the junction with the Crewe line on the left, the signalman leans from the sliding doors of his box with a wave for the driver. I am reminded of a descrip-tion by Adrian Vaughan, a former signalman who became Brunel's biographer, in his book *Signalman's Morning*:

Levers were always pulled with a duster. This prevented sweat from rusting the carefully polished steel handles and made pulling more comfortable and easier because the handle had to move in the hand, which it could not do when gripped tightly in bare fists. Not any rag did for this job, but a proper duster – a square of soft cotton cloth with red, light and dark blue lines. The design had not changed in living memory – only the initials, and even in 1960 I was the proud owner of a duster with the magic cipher GWR woven into it.

My stopping service pulls in alongside the last 'big train' of the day – the 16.07 Wrexham and Shropshire service to London Marylebone. Big, of course, is relative in this part of the world – two coaches plus a restaurant car and a DVT. (DVT stands for the inelegant 'driving van trailer' in railway jargon. Its purpose is to allow a train to be driven with the locomotive at the back.) This DVT was pensioned off from the Euston line when the Pendolinos took over in 2002 and was designed with a cavernous space for parcels but no seats for passengers. As you might expect, there are no parcels on the slow train from Shrewsbury to Marylebone this afternoon, although the DVT represents fifty tonnes of non-revenue-earning weight.

But the stewards, welcoming a handful of passengers onto the train, look important and busy in their maroon waistcoats, striding up and down the platform. A red-faced German tourist puffs up asking, 'Is this the quickest way to London?' 'Well actually, you might do better getting the next train to Birmingham and then the fast train to Euston' is the reply. But he decides to stick with the slower train, which is looking very self-important, with No. 67013 and its grand-sounding Welsh name *Dyfrbont Pontcysyllte* on the front. 'What does it mean?' I ask one of the stewards. 'Haven't a clue' is the reply. A call through to the Welsh Assembly press office later reveals it is the name of Pontcysyllite aqueduct, which I'd passed earlier in the day, and means literally the 'bridge connected to the river'.

And so we are off, heading for the capital, the hooter of *Dyfrbont Pontcysyllite* echoing off the castle walls, past the remains of the Benedictine abbey built by Roger de Montgomery, William the Conquerer's favourite lieutenant, in 1083, and wrecked not in any battle between English and Welsh but by Thomas Telford, who built the road to London, cutting the journey time from four days to sixteen hours, destroying much of the abbey in the process. A more modern monument is the great Severn Bridge Junction signal box, built by the London and North Western Railway and the largest surviving mechanical signal box in Britain, with a frame accommodating 180 levers. Many of these are no longer used, but from his perch the signalman here controls a vast network of upper quadrant, lower quadrant and colour light signals, which fortunately are set to remain operated in their quaint nineteenth-century way for the foreseeable future.

We can no longer travel on the Great Central's original main line, since much of the track on Edward Watkin's route from Nottingham to London has long been lifted. (Although a group of enthusiasts have preserved the stretch from Leicester to Loughborough as a splendid Edwardian time capsule – the only double-track preserved railway in Britain and the only place where two steam locomotives regularly pass at speed travelling in opposite directions.) Instead, we are to traverse the old Great Central's second-best line, through High Wycombe, which it built jointly with the Great Western Railway to relieve congestion on the approaches to Marylebone. This really was the last main line of the steam era. Expensively constructed, it was opened as late as 1906 and widely condemned as an imperial extravagance, already redundant at the dawn of the motor age. Yet it survived Beeching and now carries a busy service from Birmingham to London.

There are only a handful of us in the first-class restaurant car for the journey through the Chilterns on this sunny evening. Shame, since this is one of the last opportunities to dine in style on any service train in Britain. Thomas Ableman, who does the marketing for the line, is pleased with his product. He joins me for the rest of the journey, and although he appears too young to remember the nationalised railway, let alone Beeching, and with his thick-rimmed glasses looks more like a don than a railwayman, he has just seen off an attempt by rival Virgin to run their own regular service to Wrexham. This would have provided two extra trains a day but, ever sensitive to bad publicity, the canny Virgin boss Richard Branson backed off. In fact it was misleading, as some newspapers did, to portray W & S as a minnow squashed by a corporate giant, since it is part of the mighty Deutsche Bahn, the German state railway, which also owns Britain's biggest rail freight company and Chiltern Railways, the lucrative franchise that runs through the Buckinghamshire stockbroker belt into London, not to mention a half-share of the London Overground – the newest part of the Tube. And wasn't this the kind of cut-throat competition that rail privatisation was supposed to be about?

We gather speed through Wellington, with the 1,300 foot bulk of the Wrekin to the right blocking out the setting sun, and stop at Telford, where our restaurant starts to fill up with tired-looking reps, laptops under their arms and ID cards dangling like necklaces. As well as providing restaurant cars, Ableman tells me, the company's strategy has been to undercut the peak-time fares of the big operators. 'So how can you make money with just three carriages pulled by one of the thirstiest diesels on the network?' I ask him. It's called growing the market, he says.

But it's an odd sort of market. We stop at Wolverhampton but are not allowed to pick up passengers because of what are called 'moderation of competition' rules, which do not allow our tiny train to compete against bigger firms who have shelled out billions to buy their franchises. We are not permitted to stop at Birmingham at all and so are forced to rattle around the edge of the city over freight lines past endless metal-bashers' yards, to rejoin the Euston main line at Stechford, where the train has to wait for six minutes every night to allow the Birmingham to London Pendolino express to pull ahead. 'But at least it's good for the mobile phone signal,' offers Ableman. Coventry? No stopping allowed here either, so we are diverted over the branch line to Leamington. At least this line, once freight-only, has a new lease of life. But now we are able to speed up, since the only competitor on the remaining journey to London is sister company Chiltern Railways. But this is primarily a commuter line, and we have to be patient behind the Clubman multiple-unit trains shuttling their way to and from Marylebone.

But why should speed matter when we're pottering through the Chilterns, the chalk hillsides glistening golden in the setting sun, and dining from a menu that would not disgrace a top West End restaurant. I have wild mushroom soup, lamb shank in red wine and rosemary sauce, followed by chocolate torte. And, in deference to the German proprietors, I choose the Munsterer Pittersberg 2007. And yes, the food is freshly cooked on the train, Brian the steward, a dead ringer for Graham Norton, informs me. He is proud the train's staff all come from North Wales and not from the capital. 'It's where the quality is, darling,' he tells me. 'And why don't you have a teensy-weensy bit more?' I settle for the cheese board. 'Was the service all right?' he asks, taking my plate away. 'You know I sometimes let myself down like a cheap pair of braces.'

We're getting closer to London now, through Bicester, famous for the last-ever 'slip coach' operation in Britain, where expresses slipped the coupling of a single coach to cruise to a halt at a wayside station, rather than stop the main train itself. Past Princes Risborough with its old GWR signal box and the great Saunderton cutting, the last ever in Britain to be hewn by an army of navvies. Sadly we don't stop at the splendidly named Denham Golf Club station, where for all we know young men straight out of Metroland may already be drinking pink gins with their Joan Hunter-Dunns on this beautiful evening.

London is closing in fast. Here's Wembley already, where Edward Watkin started work on a grand tower that was to be 150 feet taller than the Eiffel Tower in Paris. Known as 'Watkin's Folly' it never got beyond the first tier and went ignominiously for scrap in 1907. The wine list is clearly going down well, as the Telford reps are in boisterous mood. Perhaps it doesn't matter that it has taken us three hours and fifteen minutes to get here.

It's clear how dramatically the fortunes of this last main line have changed as we draw into Marylebone's Platform 1. The canopy is blue with diesel smoke as crowded commuter trains prepare themselves for departure at five-minute intervals from what is now one of Britain's busiest stations. How different from 1971, when the historian L T C Rolt wrote, 'There was never any rush hour worthy of the name at Marylebone and no-one seemed to be in a hurry. Standing in its quiet spacious concourse, cut off from the fretful sound of the traffic in the Marylebone Road, you half expected to hear the sound of cathedral bells.' Now Marylebone is among the most confident of London termini, perhaps more so than any other apart from St Pancras, sporting two newly constructed platforms, with plans afoot to extend services to new destinations including Oxford and Aberystwyth. But still the spirit of the old Marylebone lives on amid the buzz of shops and fast-food outlets. Peer behind the bottles of Chardonnay in the Marks and Spencer Simply Food outlet on the concourse and you can see the magnificent carved mahogany windows of the old booking office. And why not toast Sir Edward Watkin with a gin and lime in the bar of the old Great Central Hotel over the road, now luxuriously reinvented as the Landmark. Watkin's critics may have considered him an extravagant dreamer. But the old boy certainly knew how to do it in style.

Postscript: the Wrexham and Shropshire Railway went abruptly out of business at the end of January 2011, citing losses of £13 million. Perhaps it was too good to be true. But it is sure to live on in memory as a paragon among modern railway services. Fortunately it is still possible to enjoy this scenic route almost in its entirety by changing trains in Birmingham. A short walk between New Street and Moor Street Stations is necessary, but there is ample compensation in the splendidly restored Great Western Railway buildings at the latter, which recreate the elegant atmosphere of an Edwardian railway terminus.

Steely heritage: Ex-LMS 'Class 4F' No. 44347 heads a special
train past Millom Ironworks on the Cumbrian Coast line in August 1961.
The industry has vanished and the site where the furnaces stood
is now a bird sanctuary.

CHAPTER FIVE

THE 08.38 TO SELLAFIELD – A JOURNEY ALONG THE LINE THAT TIME FORGOT

Preston to Carlisle, via Grange-over-Sands,
Barrow-in-Furness, Ravenglass, Sellafield,
Workington and Maryport

Some of the most splendid hotels in the land were originally station hotels – and some still are: the Landmark in Marylebone, the Midland in Manchester, the Queen's in Leeds. However, I'm in the Station Hotel in Millom, on the west coast of the Lake District. Splendid is a word few people might readily use – and as far as Lakeland scenery goes, there are no hosts of golden daffodils to be seen for miles around. Richard, the proprietor, had already warned me. 'I ought to tell you,' he said when I phoned through my booking. 'It might look like the Lake District on the map, but I don't want you to get a surprise.' The local lads are screeching round in beat-up Nissans outside, doing handbrake turns; a double vodka and Red Bull is £3.99 in the bar. What was once the town's department store is derelict and boarded up. Even the Job Centre is up for sale. 'We never recovered since the steelworks closed in 1968,' says Alicia, the waitress in the Da Vinci restaurant. 'This is the last eating place in town since the Thai closed,' she tells me as she dishes up a pizza margherita. The big local employer these days is Haverigg Prison.

I'd already been briefed about Millom by John Kitchen, who looks after the local railway lines for Cumbria Council. I had no choice but to break my journey there on the slowest of slow trains along the Cumbrian coast because all the Lake District hotels in this hot, high summer week were full. 'Well, take Millom as you find it,' he said. 'But I promise you, there is no other rail journey in Britain as good as this one.' What can he mean? By his reckoning, it is the most scenic coastal railway in England and the least discovered by tourism. Quite a claim, since Britain's most famous stretches of coastal railway – from Durham to Berwick on the East Coast Main Line and along the Great Western main line at Dawlish in Devon – are regularly voted the most attractive in the land.

The Cumbrian Coast line is also among the slowest, swinging in a great arc for 114 miles from Carnforth in Lancashire to Carlisle, sandwiched for most of the way between the Lakeland fells and the Irish Sea. By the time my 08.38 train from Preston to Carlisle plods its way to its destination, I could have travelled to London and back again. The Cumbrian Coast line is the last survivor of a cat's cradle of lines built to service the ironworks and coal mines of West Cumbria. Beeching finished off most of them and Margaret Thatcher in the 1980s did for the rest. Don't take this trip if you're planning to change your mind anywhere along the line. There are no branches; local bus routes are sparse: and you might have to book a taxi twenty-four hours in advance to get to the next village. Bluntly, there is no way out. In the era of the TGV and the Bullet Train, this is the quintessential slow train, and intending passengers must be prepared for something of an adventure.

So obscure is it that there is no consensus on the line in the tourist literature. Is it just a route, as some say, through a string of ugly towns which look as though they have been deposited like flotsam by some unusually high tide to disfigure the perimeter of Lakeland? Or is it a romantic survivor from a pre-Beeching age, with sensational views across an azure sea to the hills of south-west Scotland from one side of the train and of the dramatic crags of Wainwright country on the other? Either way, the Cumbrian Coast line is a near-complete survivor of a secondary railway from the golden age. Station gardens are still tended, station buildings are mostly intact, even if many are disused or converted into homes. Semaphore signals creak and clatter up and down, and at almost every halt is a little wooden signal box, where the signaller taps a bell announcing he is letting the train through to the next section. Above all the line still possesses the sense of community that defined the railways in the pre-Beeching era and is now almost extinct. This really is the railway that time forgot.

So, as the train from Preston swings off the main line to Scotland at Carnforth, there is no turning back. Despite having become a kind of *Brief Encounter* theme park with the famous tearooms and clock restored, no main line trains stop at Carnforth any longer, so a modern-day Trevor and Celia would probably have to jump aboard our two-car Class 156 Sprinter unit – a decidedly non-romantic diesel train dating from the British Rail era. At each stop the engines rev themselves into a frenzy before deciding reluctantly and noisily to propel the train into motion. Not much sprinting here. But at least the windows are clean and they can be opened for ventilation. Don't ever do a journey like this on an early BR train that claims to have air conditioning, I have been warned. And there are other potential horrors: Class 142 Pacer trains, built from old Leyland bus parts and known as 'nodding donkeys' because they buck up and down so much on the uneven track are banned from the line now. But the operator, Northern Rail, is not awash with money. It is the most heavily subsidised of all the train companies and the Cumbrian Coast is hardly top of the priority list. So the Pacers have a habit of reappearing when they are least expected. Today is Carlisle race day, and John Kitchen has sent the control room a warning about overcrowding. 'You wouldn't want to stand on one of those things all the way up from Whitehaven,' he tells me. Even so, it's not long before our train passes a dilapidated-looking Pacer on the southbound track.

What a contrast with the India-red steam locomotives of the Victorian Furness Railway, with their comfy ultramarine blue and white carriages, which once came this way. Luckily, Locomotive No. 3 *Old Coppernob*, dating from 1843, is preserved in the National Railway Museum, York, although it was the victim of a sensational theft when its numberplate was stolen under the noses of museum staff in 2008. But never mind. There is plenty of Furness Railway heritage to be seen in the well-preserved stations at the little resorts developed by the railway company around Morecambe Bay as we cross from Lancaster into Cumbria. Spot the squirrels tucking into bunches of grapes on the cast-iron platform seat ends. They are collector's items, much sought after by enthusiasts. Even the names are evocative of this rustic coastline – Silverdale, Arnside, Ulverston.

Arnside station is the starting point for the famous Morecambe Bay walk – a four-mile trek across treacherous shifting sands. If you ask him nicely, the Queen's Guide to the Sands, a local fisherman, will lead you across. The high point of the journey is wading through the River Kent – the first of five rivers whose waters flow down to the Cumbrian Coast. But no wading is needed if you are on the train – the trip over the Kent Viaduct has been described as like skimming the waters on a seaplane. Ever since it was built, the railway around the edge of Morecambe Bay has always trumped the road route, with no need to divert round the little estuaries. The train progresses in a lordly way past mysterious Holme Island, its secrets protected by a shroud of trees which conceal a full-size copy of the Temple of Vesta in Rome. John Brogden, the consultant engineer who built the line, once lived here, but today the iron gates on the causeway are firmly and intriguingly padlocked. An odd place, since when the tide is out the island is surrounded not by sand but by the invasive spartina grass, now causing an ecological problem as it runs wild in Morecambe Bay.

Some passengers are baffled about the prettiness of the line as we head around the bay towards Barrow-in-Furness. Shouldn't there be some furnaces here, or at least the odd steelworks? 'Don't get confused about the name,' says Peter Anderson, a retired council planner who is president of the Cumbrian Railways Association. 'Furness has got nothing to do with furnaces. It actually means father of Ness.' Anderson, who leads a band of more than 400 enthusiasts from as far away as South Wales dedicated to supporting the line, meets me on the platform at Grange-over-Sands and briefs me over a pot of tea in the ever-so-genteel Cedar Tea Rooms. 'No minstrels or anything of the noisy order,' proclaimed the 1906 edition of the *Guide to Seaside Places* in its entry on Grange. Clearly not much has changed in this resort, where feeding the ducks in the municipal gardens seems as exciting as it gets.

Even in Barrow, whose fortunes really were built on steel, there are not many furnaces these days, Anderson explains. You are more likely to encounter protectively clad engineers from the nuclear industry. But iron and coal run through the veins, literally, of West Cumbria, and through the veins of the men who developed it. Iron was first discovered by the Romans, Anderson tells me, as he pours the tea, and by the year 1200 was being mined by the monks of St Bees Priory along the coast. It was the reason for the development of a tangle of wonderfully named railways in the area – the Maryport and Carlisle, the Whitehaven and Furness Junction, the Ravenglass and Eskdale and the Cockermouth, Keswick and Penrith. Giants of the Industrial Revolution stalked the land round here. George Stephenson, designer of the *Rocket*, was appointed by his friend William Lowther, second Earl of Lonsdale, to link the Lowther family's mines and factories in Whitehaven to the national rail network in Carlisle. His ancestor Sir John Lowther was known as the 'richest commoner in England' and built his factory chimneys in the shape of his favourite silver candlesticks. But two of Britain's greatest inventors defined the prosperity of the area and its railways. One was the Cumbrian John Wilkinson, who discovered a way of replacing charcoal with common coal for smelting. Henry Bessemer was an even more prolific genius, inventing a process that could transform pig iron into steel. There was no better ingredient than pure Cumbrian haematite, and for more than a century Workington, a few stations up the line, exported rolled steel track to build railways far and wide across the world. Sadly, it went the way of much of British industry, and Workington's rail-making works, which first exported to the Texas and Alabama Railway in 1872, were finally closed in 2006.

We're now into our second cup of Assam, and discussing the merits of the Italianate style of the local station architecture – with nice touches such as the monogram of the Furness Railway set into the cast-iron lamp holders. Grange station is especially attractive, and a plaque on the wall pronounces it WINNER. BEST INTERNATIONAL SMALL STATION OF THE YEAR 2007. Another grander plaque says the station was built in 1872 to the design of James Brunlees and is a replica of the top storey of the Grange Hotel. 'This is quite wrong,' says Anderson, who clearly knows as much about the line as it is possible to know. But the next train is due, and life is slow enough on the Cumbrian Coast for me not to be able to afford to miss it. The train is surprisingly full as we rumble over the next estuary crossing and onto the Leven Viaduct, an even grander piece of engineering than the Kent Viaduct, recently rebuilt by Network Rail, who closed the line for four months during its reconstruction. In 1903 the Whitehaven to Carnforth Mail was blown over here, though fortunately not into the water. But the passengers were left to crawl to safety on their hands and knees through the storm. There was even greater drama farther along the line at Lindal, where the engine of a goods train disappeared into a hole opened up by mining subsidence. It was never recovered, an intact piece of industrial archaeology frozen in time and waiting to be exhumed by generations hence.

The views are especially lovely here, as the line weaves through the Vale of Nightshade and past the remains of Furness Abbey, built by the Cistercians and second only in importance to Fountains Abbey in Yorkshire. The construction of the railway infuriated William Wordsworth, who called the company's direc- tors 'profane despoilers'. He had already publicly warmed to the theme with a sonnet attacking the building of a new line to Windermere. 'Is there no nook of English ground secure from rash assault?' he wrote. One wonders what he would have made of the hideous rectangular bulk of Heysham nuclear power sta- tion, which disfigures many of the views from our train window along this part of the coast.

It seems incredible that during the nineteenth century the directors of the Furness turned the docks at Barrow into England's third-largest after London and Liverpool. In modern times the ship-yards were renowned as the place where Britain's Trident nuclear submarines were built. But the naval industry fell on hard times at the end of the Cold War and there is not so much reason to come here now: the last direct trains to London Euston were withdrawn in the 1980s. As one commentator observed, 'There were not enough submarine salesmen journeying to the consulates and embassies of the capital to justify a through service.' Building nuclear submarines is hardly a vote winner these days and the number of people working in the shipyards is a fraction of what it once was. In any case, the town has other claims to fame. In 2002 it suffered the world's fourth-biggest outbreak of legionnaires' disease in which seven people died. In 2008 it was judged the most working-class town in Britain, something of a contrast with the 1870s, when it had the largest number of aristocrats per head of any town in the land. While the train is waiting I alight briefly to use the gentlemen's toilet, which I discover to be the cleanest I have ever seen on a railway station. Could there be a connection?

'Where do you want to get off?' asks Brian, the conductor. North from Barrow is the least used section of the line and many of the stations are request stops. Brian seems constantly to be popping his head round the driver's door to let him know. He tells me that one conductor at Carlisle got into trouble for announcing, 'All stations to Whitehaven and beyond – though why anybody would want to get off there, I have no idea.' Today I have a very good idea of where I want to alight. I am planning to stop for lunch at Foxfield on the edge of the sands of the Duddon estuary, where I'm joining the lunchtime crowd at the Prince of Wales, a legendary local boozer opposite the station. Its fame in brewing its own real ales extends far beyond Cumbria. The City editor of a London newspaper, well versed in the fare of the finest private dining rooms of the Square Mile, told me he considers the Prince of Wales, Foxfield a 'paradise on earth'.

I tell this to Brian, who says, 'Sometimes we get trainfuls of thirsty blokes travelling up the line at lunchtime for the pub. We pick them up legless on the last train home. But doesn't do any harm, does it? They're mostly nice people. And what else is there to do round here since the Millom steelworks closed?' Brian, who is sixty-two, tells me he comes from Ipswich and taught in local schools for sixteen years before he joined the railway three years ago.

You get mostly nicer people on the train than I generally encountered in teaching. But shame they took the passenger services off the Foxfield to Coniston branch back in 1958. They didn't even hang around till Beeching came along. Said it was losing £16,000 a year – does that sound like a lot to you? One day they came along and just closed it, just like that. It was the prettiest branch line in Britain. You could have changed at Foxfield and gone right up to the lake. Now the cars are just nose to tail on the local roads – they can't pack any more in. They had special little steam-powered carriages with big windows so you could see the scenery more easily. You know, the writer John Ruskin would have gone this way – he had a place up at Coniston.

I wonder how much the fastidious Ruskin would have enjoyed a pint or two of Good Old Boy ale among the amply gutted men in 'Coniston Beer Festival' T-shirts at the bar of the Prince of Wales, although aesthetics are not on the agenda as I attempt a House Special Giant Pasty with mushy peas and a pint of Foxfield Old Pale. He would at least have been close enough to the platform to jump aboard the next branch train to Coniston, where he would almost certainly have admired the Swiss-chalet-style station. There's a grand view of the signalman in his box here, kitted out with an array of levers fit to control a country junction, complete with water tower to fill the boilers of steam engines but without much more to do than control a level crossing and a farm track. The signal box, perched on top of a little weatherboarded waiting room, looks as though it might fall down of its own accord. A crumpled-up Somerfield plastic bag is stuffed in the window frame where the wood has rotted away. But the view from here, across the serene waters of the Duddon estuary, must be one of the most beautiful from a railway station anywhere in Britain.

Like the Foxfield–Coniston route, almost all the branch lines into the heart of the Lake District are now fading memories. The Lakeside branch from Ulverston, a few stops back along the line before Barrow, was killed off by Beeching in 1965 just four years before its centenary, although the northern section from Haverthwaite was saved by a group of enthusiasts and now operates as a heritage line, with some authentic former London, Midland and Scottish Railway Fairburn tank engines, the last of their kind still running. Further north, the line that passed through Keswick on its way from Workington to Penrith, and the only one to traverse the Lakes from east to west, was an even more tragic casualty of the 1960s closures, drawing fury from locals as Beeching had his way. The first section west of Keswick went in 1966, the trackbed being turned over to the builders of the new A66 road, and the rest went soon after.

But the little narrow-gauge line from Ravenglass, along beautiful Eskdale to Dalegarth, at the foot of England's highest mountains, lives on. 'La'al Ratty', as the Ravenglass and Eskdale is known locally, is probably the only profitable secondary railway in Cumbria, and one of the few profitable non-nuclear enterprises on this part of the Cumbrian Coast. It takes my train just twenty-eight minutes to get here from Foxfield, and crossing the platform to change trains you can see why the Ratty is so successful. Two miniature replicas of mainline steam locomotives sit simmering in the sidings. The one that is to haul my train seven miles into the heart of the Lakes is the mustard-coloured *River Irt*, which, according to a notice on the platform, was 'built in 1894, the oldest working 15-inch gauge locomotive in the world'. Being swung round on the turntable is her sister, the *River Mite*, painted in the India red of the Furness Railway. She looks like the fastest and most thrilling express engine in the world, but you have to get down on your knees and half close your eyes to imagine it.

But this is no toy railway; it operates throughout the year, carrying both locals and tourists. The Ravenglass and Eskdale was opened in 1875 to carry quarried haematite down to the Furness Railway main line, as well as the occasional passenger. But when supplies of the ore started to run out, it was rescued as the realisation of a grown-up little boy's dream. The saviour was a Northampton model maker called Wynne Bassett-Lowke. (The firm had a famous model shop in High Holborn, a mecca for young boys and their fathers until it closed in the 1970s.) Bassett-Lowke rebuilt the line changing the gauge from 3 feet to 15 inches. Since then La'al Ratty has gone from strength to strength. Some of its success may be due to the fact that it is one of the few non-imaginary railways to be enshrined in the Thomas the Tank Engine canon. The 'Arlesdale Railway' in the Reverend W Awdrey's *Small Railway Engines* is based on the Ravenglass and Eskdale, where Awdrey spent a holiday with his clergyman chum the Reverend E R Boston; they take the parts of the 'Thin Clergyman' and the 'Fat Clergyman' respectively.

And what a jolly ride the two clerics must have had on the train up the valley. Today, in the open-top carriages, families with young children sucking on Starbursts mingle with stern-looking hikers in Tilley hats, shorts and Hillmasters – 'Scafell Pike, here we come!' There is even space for bikes. 'You can sit in one of the open carriages,' Geoffrey the volunteer ticket collector tells me. 'But don't dance on the ceiling!' Ho-ho! Warm steam blows back in our faces as the *River Irt* chuffs past giant ferns and oaks, her carriages emitting a curious *da-da-tiddlypop, da-da-tiddlypop*. An upturned boat serves as a station shelter at Murthwaite. Here a red squirrel is briefly glimpsed scampering away from the train, while a buzzard hovers menacingly above the valley. The dark presence of Harter Fell, 2,129 feet, looms on the right. And then *whoomph* as the brakes suddenly go on, followed by the staccato *bish-bosh* of the Westinghouse brakes on the loco. It turns out that a flock of the local Herdwick sheep, with their curious black coats, have strayed onto the track, and the driver has to climb down to shoo them off.

Back at Ravenglass station there is a crowd quaffing Ratty Ale in the Ratty Arms, part of the miniature railway's empire, which has taken over much of the old Furness Railway station. The workshops are in the goods shed and the museum and pub are in the station buildings on opposite platforms. The sun is sinking over the Mite Estuary as the *River Irt* is put to bed in the engine shed, and I wait for the last train of the day to my own berth in the Millom Station hotel. Quarter past seven doesn't seem late for a last train, but clearly Northern Rail expects its customers to be tucked up early. (No clubbing round here, please.) But I wait half an hour, and no train appears. Then forty-five-minutes have gone, and I look around at the once-busy scene to find everything shut and no one to ask. No hotel vacancies round here in picturesque Ravenglass, which is why I'm slumming it in Millom. I think of Edward Thomas's 'Adlestrop': 'No one came and no one went on the bare platform . . .' Perhaps I shall have to walk. But then I remember not Adlestrop but Bangalore, and use my mobile phone to ring the nice lady at National Rail Enquiries head-quarters in India. 'Your train is running precisely forty-nine minutes late,' she tells me, consulting her computer screen and beaming back the news across the world to Cumbria. 'But supposing I didn't have a mobile phone,' I say to her. 'How could I have known?' There's a crackly silence at the end of the line.

When the southbound train finally arrives, the conductor is apologetic.

A few days ago we had a Class 153 [single-carriage] train come off the track near Dalston. There were seventeen aboard and lucky none of them were injured. They reckon it was a rail that buckled in the heat. I spoke to the driver and he said it drifted off the rails into the ballast, just like that. They're playing safe today and slowing us all up. They like to call us a 'showpiece line'. But do you think it really is? The real problem is the trains. They're too short and we haven't got enough of them. Sometimes I get twelve cyclists wanting to get aboard at Whitehaven, where the Coast-to-Coast Path starts. They get a bit iffy when they say I can't let them all on. And don't talk to me about the Pacers . . .

At Millom the darkened station is deserted and the bar at the Station Hotel is empty. The barmaid is resting on her elbows watching TV, and there seem to be no takers for the cheapo deal on vodka and Red Bull. Still, I get a good night's sleep before resuming the journey north along the line the next morning. But first I have something to seek out – the little house at 14 St George's Terrace where the poet Norman Nicholson, the 'modern bard of the Lake District', was born and lived for most of his life. His poetry more than anything sums up the schizophrenic nature of the Cumbrian Coast railway's hinterland. I interviewed him just before he died in 1987 and he said something that I have never forgotten – that the rock that forms the noble high fells of Cumbria is the same rock that put bread on the table for thousands of families through the mines and quarries and iron-works.

Millom's once-mighty Hodbarrow steelworks is now a memory and its bulldozed site is a bird sanctuary – home to the rare great-crested grebe, once almost extinct in Britain. The only industries that put bread on the table for local people these days are the vast facilities run by the Nuclear Decommissioning Authority (formerly British Nuclear Fuels Ltd) along the 'nuclear coast'. Millom station platform this morning is thronged with Sellafield-bound passengers, and looks more like rush hour in suburban south-east England than one of the most depressed towns in Britain. 'It's a fact,' says the lady who runs the Millom Folk Museum in the old station booking office, 'that Millom is the busiest station in the UK. You work it out by comparing the number of people who use the trains with the population. Footfall, they call it.'

I ponder this as the packed train heads towards Sellafield, where the vast cooling towers and chimneys dominate the landscape for miles around. Even the names of the local stations have a sinister ring. Drigg, for instance, sounds as though God could have created it for the purpose of storing nuclear waste. Ten thousand people, nearly all of them local, are employed in Sellafield and its related plants, and while international environmentalists would like to see the whole place closed down, the locals will have none of it, believing it to be entirely good for their economic, if not physical, health. The original name Windscale was changed to Sellafield after a major fire in 1957 led to a core meltdown and the discharge of vast amounts of radioactive material into the local landscape and the Irish Sea. Another leak from the Thorp reprocessing plant in 2005 went undetected for nine months. Even according to the management, building B30, in the heart of the facility, is the most hazardous industrial building in Europe. Now another giant nuclear power station is to be built on the coast here with enough power to meet the energy needs of Leeds, Cardiff and Glasgow combined. Yet nobody seems fazed. The railway station at Drigg has a splendid platform garden full of pre-nuclear age delights such as roses, antirrhinums, delphiniums and petunias tended by the lady from the gift shop next door. She even has a home-made set of steps to help passengers from the trains – it is not deemed economic to rebuild the low Furness Railway platforms. Just down the road is Britain's main low-level nuclear waste dump, although let's not dwell on it now.

In the sidings near Sellafield station I count eight flasks of spent nuclear waste from power stations all over the nation. Enough nuclear material here, mixed in the right cocktail, for a new Hiroshima and much more than is at the disposal of the presidents of Iran and North Korea, yet yards away workers are nonchalantly playing golf on an immaculate green in the shadow of the cooling towers. 'They're some of the best players in the world,' the man opposite me on the train remarks, 'because they've got six fingers on each hand!' Somehow everything seems sinister here when it's really perfectly mundane. I start to wonder why two watering cranes for filling steam locomotives have been retained on the platform, nearly half a century after steam ended. Conspiracy theorists might ponder on a low-tech evacuation – or did they just forget to take them away? Certainly the ranks of cormorants and herring gulls lined up on the beach like sentries look as fit and spruce as can be.

The line becomes single track most of the way to Whitehaven from here, hugging the coast, and in the days when you could open carriage windows in trains you could almost reach out and touch the sea. No road anywhere in Britain takes you so close to the waves for so long. Domesticity reasserts itself at Seascale, once intended by the Furness directors to be, like Grange-over-Sands, a 'Torquay of the North'. But only one hotel was brave enough to open and the town is little more than a few grey houses clustered around an expanse of featureless beach. It's a tough choice which side of the train to sit for the finest views. The railway staff say they never tire of the moods of the sea here, whether the smooth azure ocean of July or the vicious grey sea of winter, when huge waves sometimes crash over the tracks. But the views of the Lakeland fells on the land side of the train are just as exciting – Seatallan, Haycock, Pillar and High Stile pass by in procession – though never be surprised to encounter a forest of wind turbines round the next bend. There is hardly a stretch of the route from Silverdale to Maryport where lazily rotating fins are not visible somewhere on the horizon.

Along the beach is a community of shanty dwellers, whose homes bear names such as Sea Breeze and Peacehaven. Legend has it that under the roofing felt and weatherboarding with which most of them are covered are some original Furness Railway carriages. A goods train once rolled off the embankment here, crushing many of them, but fortunately their inhabitants were out at the time. The shacks extend nearly as far as St Bees, where on this sunny morning elegant schoolgirls in whites are playing tennis in the shadow of the medieval priory, where the organ is famous for its 2,000 pipes.

'It's not always so peaceful,' the guard tells me. 'The boys go into Whitehaven for supplies of alcohol, which they smuggle in their rooms. Sometimes they get back on the train swigging from two-litre bottles of White Ice cider. It's like industrial fuel, and you could fire up Sellafield with it. The kids are rowdier than the grown-up drunks a lot of the time!' I ask him for a request stop at Parton, a bleak little former smelting village, but with sensational views along the coast. From here I plan to take the Cumbria Coast Path back to Whitehaven, the most important town on the line. 'Oh, you mean Dolly's nipple,' he says, cheerily referring to the fact that the train rounds a promontory. The line here is known as 'Avalanche Alley', owing to the frequent landslides caused by the unstable geology of the cliffs and the colliery workings on the cliff top. Rails can become buckled overnight or even carried away by the sea. Three separate slips sometimes occur within forty-eight hours, placing this stretch of line very much between the devil and the deep blue sea. But for passengers who venture this far, there are fewer more thrilling rides in the whole of Europe.

Whitehaven is cheery and breezy in the sunshine, slowly rein-venting itself after years of industrial decline. In the eighteenth century it was the third-biggest port in England, exporting coal in exchange for rum and tobacco. These days the only rum to be seen is in the carrier bags of the yachties, whose boats have replaced the coasters in the harbour. The town's main claim to fame is that it was the last place in England to be invaded – by the pirate John Paul Jones in 1788 – and is also reckoned to have the third-largest number of Georgian houses in the country. But Whitehaven is clearly struggling with the burden of its heritage. A piece of the lettering has fallen off the sign of the John Paul Jones pub, and the loveliest Georgian building in the town is a pizza takeaway.

Whitehaven's station is one of only two that are staffed in the eighty-four miles between Barrow and Carlisle, and this after-noon there is a notice in the booking office: SORRY WE ARE

CLOSED. Not much to miss here: the Victorian station buildings were demolished in 1980 to be replaced by a Tesco supermarket and a soulless little booking office, although a grand signal box named Whitehaven Bransty remains as a reminder of busier times. The bus station opposite is also closed and derelict, though part of it is occupied by a Wetherspoon's pub. So I'm off down the line to Workington, where I find the charming Alastair Grey, the booking clerk – labelled 'Travel Adviser' in modern railspeak – who is only too happy to show me round. Workington is the only station on the line with most of its original Victorian buildings and canopies intact, although they are now quietly mouldering and in need of several licks of paint. Grass grows high between the flagstones, although the atmosphere is charming – a branch line junction frozen in time. Even the fast lines running through the middle of the station are intact, though it is decades since any fast trains ran here, let alone any trains needing to overtake others. The warren of rooms on the platforms that once served as parcels offices, ladies' waiting rooms, lamp rooms and places for the dispatch of pigeons are shuttered and empty. Hard to believe you could once board the Lakes Express direct to Euston from here, or that porters would pace the platforms crying 'All change for Keswick and stations beyond' as ladies with Rowney sketch pads took the little branch train that pirouetted Swiss-style over viaducts and through tunnels high on the hillsides to reach the heart of the Lake District. The Lakes Express survived until the closure of the branch line in the 1960s, and held the distinction of being the only express train in the country running alongside a lake, skirting Bassenthwaite Lake for three miles. I wonder if the wobbly foxgloves still surviving in Workington's long-neglected station garden might date from those days.

'We're doing really well at the moment,' Alastair tells me. 'Thirty per cent up on passenger numbers compared with last year. People are catching on to how beautiful the line is.' Though it's a far cry from the days when the steelworks were at full blast and the freight sidings were humming. 'It was a blow when we lost the Travelling Post Office back in 1991, though we still get one freight a day – of china clay down to the docks. The problem for us was that the Settle and Carlisle got all the publicity when they tried to close it, and we somehow got left out. Look at this!' He shows me blackened mildew weeping down the plaster in the booking office wall. But he has pledged to get some restoration under way. 'I used to be on the buses, you know, but there's no better life than on the railway – even today. It only takes me fifteen minutes to cycle to work in the mornings. I love it here.'

Alastair sees me off on the next train to Carlisle, promising it will be better next time I come. As we head for Maryport you can spy the cloud-covered hills of Galloway across the Solway Firth – looking in the early evening like a mystical floating island. From here Mary Queen of Scots fled in an open boat to Cumberland, from where she wrote her famous letter to Elizabeth I seeking forgiveness. The Scottish coast here was one of the locations for the shooting of the cult film *The Wicker Man*, starring Edward Woodward and Christopher Lee. From Maryport the train turns away from the coast into a primarily agricultural landscape, where fat brown cattle lord it over the landscape. Not all is bucolic bliss, however: at Wigton, birthplace of the critic and novelist Lord Bragg, the giant Innovia cellophane plant seethes and fumes next to the railway. But, like Sellafield, it is a very welcome employer.

As we rattle across the junction to join the main line into Carlisle there is, to the left of the tracks an elegant reminder of the line's heritage, a large Victorian sandstone warehouse bearing the legend MARYPORT AND CARLISLE GOODS AND COAL DEPOT in black and white capitals along the roof. Sadly it has been partly obliterated by a large ugly polystyrene sign advertising 'Sleepright, the Bed Store'.

Beauty accompanied by blight. On the Cumbrian Coast line it is mostly inevitable. But as Norman Nicholson might have said, it makes the journey all the more worth taking.

Age of elegance: The Golden Arrow at London's
Victoria station in 1957. With its luxurious Pullman cars and
fine dining, the London–Paris service was always among
the most glamorous of trains.

CHAPTER SIX

THE 11.24 FROM VICTORIA – A DAY EXCURSION TO NOSTALGIA CENTRAL

*London Victoria to Canterbury and back,
via Maidstone, Ashford, Dover, and Folkestone*

This is a journey not just into the history of the railways in Britain, but also into the heart of a very British obsession. I'm settled into an armchair in Pullman coach 'Victoria' on Platform 2 of London's Victoria station. Champagne is about to be served, and the smell of a late breakfast is wafting down from the kitchen car. Of all the departure platforms in all the stations in Britain, this one is probably the most hallowed. It was once the famous 'Gateway to the Continent', from where glamorous trains to far-off places, such as the Golden Arrow and the Night Ferry, used to depart. Once, when passengers passed through the barrier here there would be connections to thrilling and exotic destinations, such as Riga, Warsaw, Bucharest, Belgrade, Sofia and Stamboul. The Golden Arrow, with its umber-and-cream art deco coaches, was the travel mode of choice to the Continent for a host of politicians, film stars and celebrities. Winston Churchill, Maurice Chevalier, Noël Coward and Marlene Dietrich used to be regular customers. The Night Ferry was a favourite of the Duke of Windsor and Mrs Simpson. Who knew what double agent, film star, diplomat or billionaire might be snuggling up in the sleeping compartment next to yours?

This morning's 11.24 Cathedrals Express departure is heading for the rather less exotic destination of Canterbury in Kent, and I doubt whether there are any spies, exiled royalty or even D-list celebrities aboard. And, in fairness, it is an exaggeration to describe it as an express, since we are to take a leisurely canter through the back routes and byways of the Garden of England before returning along the main line from Dover at less than half the speed of a Eurostar. But the glitzy heritage of the Cathedrals Express is authentic enough. Simmering on the front, all Brunswick-green and buffed up brass, is Britannia Class Locomotive No. 70013 *Oliver Cromwell*, whose classmates *Iron Duke* and *William Shakespeare* were regulars on the Golden Arrow back in the 1950s. And No. 70013, one of only two surviving representatives of the last class of express passenger engines to be built in Britain, has its own place in the pantheon, as one of the engines that pulled Britain's final steam passenger train in normal revenue-earning service on 11 August 1968 – the so-called 'Fifteen Guinea Special'. It was nicknamed thus because of the high price of the tickets, which many felt excluded ordinary railway enthusiasts. Now *Oliver Cromwell* is one of the 'people's locomotives', part of Britain's national collection, and the air at Victoria this morning is thick with nostalgia.

A curious thing this, since many of the 450 passengers on board the thirteen-coach train are too young to recall the era of steam on the railways. Most, I suspect, have no interest in rivets, nor have ever owned an Ian Allan *ABC* spotters' book, let alone stood at the end of a platform collecting numbers. Yet there is a kind of thrill in the air, a sense of expectancy that vanished from the modern railway almost half a century ago. In 2009 there were more than 270 steam-hauled excursion trains a bit like ours today (although not always so luxurious) running on the main lines of Britain. In fact, there is more steam on British main lines than in any other country in the world, and that doesn't include the preserved heritage railways, which themselves operate more mileage than the entire London Underground. This may be fitting for the nation that invented the railways but doesn't quite explain the lasting attraction. You can take your pick from the modest Shakespeare Express, shuttling between Birmingham and Stratford-upon-Avon on a summer weekend, to the ultra-luxurious Orient Express, where the cost of a single day out in 1920s Pullman coaches can buy you half a dozen easyJet tickets to wherever you fancy in Europe.

We must not mistake the Cathedrals Express for an excursion for railway enthusiasts – we are as far away from the world of anoraks, Thermos flasks and pork pies as we can get. So what is the attraction for the passengers? 'The connection between the sight of a railway engine' and a 'quite deep feeling of satisfaction is very real for multitudes of people, but it excludes rational analysis,' wrote the railway historian Roger Lloyd. But does it? I prefer the more straightforward explanation by the engineer and writer L T C Rolt:

> Of all man's mechanical inventions, the steam locomotive remains the most evocative of power and speed; it differs from more recent inventions whose design and function are of a different order, intelligible only to the technician; complicated machines which can fascinate the engineer as technical tours de force, but which lack that quality which appeals to our aesthetic sense and stirs the imagination of the layman. It is because the railways possess this quality to a unique degree that all the seven ages of man may sometimes be seen at the head of the platform to witness the departure of the express train.

Most of the ages of man seem to be at Victoria station this morning, as we pull out on time with a great cloud of steam from the cylinders immersing curious office workers, railway staff in high-visibility jackets and slightly astonished tourists at the platform end. A Rastafarian hoists his son onto his shoulders for a better view, while a young Muslim girl in a hijab takes a snap with her mobile phone. If anything can make Victoria station seem grand then it is the Cathedrals Express as it eclipses a host of unremarkable electric trains arriving and departing for the suburbs and the south coast. John Betjeman described Victoria as 'a happy sort of muddle'. It is certainly among the most confusing of London termini – the two separate stations built by the London, Brighton and South Coast Railway and the South Eastern and Chatham Railway have never quite melded into one, and for most of the day commuters from Kent bluster into trippers from Brighton, and suitcase-weary travellers from the Gatwick Express tangle with journalists from the *Daily Telegraph*, whose state-of-the-art newsroom is on a concrete platform above the station.

But all is calm now in Pullman car 'Victoria' as we accelerate across the Thames, over Grosvenor Bridge and through the cat's cradle of lines that weaves into and out of Clapham Junction. Here's the shell of Battersea Power Station, which had its heart ripped out by property developers who failed to turn it into a theme park after its closure in the 1970s and still stands abandoned and spooky – an occasional setting for the odd Grand Guignol movie. And look, there's Battersea Dogs' Home, recently expanded into feline territory with a new refuge called Cattersea. 'Just watch *Oliver Cromwell* climbing up there round the curve. Get your camera out – it'll make a great picture.' This is Marcus Robertson, boss of Steam Dreams, the company that runs the Cathedrals Express, arguably the most successful of the main line steam operators, which for a decade has run dozens of excursions each year from London. The mid-morning departure to Canterbury operates regularly during the summer. Although Robertson himself would resist being described as one, a small group of rich and slightly eccentric men have kept steam going on the main line since *Oliver Cromwell* made its valedictory 1968 trip. Unlike private heritage railways, which may be seen as the equivalent of a Hornby toy train set, running steam on the main line is more akin to collecting Bugattis or owning thoroughbred racehorses – you need nerves of steel and a bottomless pocket.

Those who know Robertson describe him as a true English eccentric who never quite outgrew his childhood – his mother is the writer Elisabeth Beresford, who created *The Wombles*, and his father Max Robertson, the veteran BBC tennis commentator. But he is also a shrewd businessman – one of a rare breed who make money doing what they love. He sold his stake in the sports sponsorship company he created with the legendary cricket commentator John Arlott to form Steam Dreams, and instead of sitting in an office can generally be found chatting to the passengers on the variety of trains he runs each week. 'My bed-room when I was a little boy,' he tells me, 'overlooked the main line from Waterloo to the West Country and all I wanted to do up to the age of eleven was to watch the steam trains go by. The big green Pacifics on trains like the Bournemouth Belle and Atlantic Coast Express were the most exciting thing ever to me. I suppose it was a seed planted then that came to fruition forty years later. But I'm not a railwayman and I'm not a trainspotter – I'm a marketing man and I spotted a gap in the market.' (He breaks off to ask the steward why one of the passengers has got black pudding but no sausages with her breakfast.) 'I suppose when my children came along and I took them on some steam trips, I realised this could have been done a lot better. Even forty years after the end of steam, the general public, who are not gricers [number collectors], love the idea of going on a trip behind a steam loco. But nobody was running anything much that appealed to ordinary people, it was all for hard-core enthusiasts.'

The train clanks to a halt at Bromley South in the heart of suburbia to pick up some more passengers – mostly silver-haired and well-heeled, I note. Robertson squints at his watch. 'Marvellous, we're on time.' He goes on: 'I wish I could claim the name Steam Dreams for myself, but I got half a dozen people from my PR firm around a table and had a brainstorm of names, and a young guy there came up with it. Do you know we were just about the first operator since BR to run timetabled steam on the main line? Can you imagine it – running steam spliced in with commuter trains in the rush hour? Back in the early 1990s this was totally unheard of.'

In fact it is fortunate that there is any steam running at all now. When *Oliver Cromwell*'s fire was put out at the end of that fateful day in 1968, British Rail imposed a total ban on steam on the main lines, even quiet ones like this rural route through West Malling to Maidstone East. Even though many of the trains and stations at the time were notoriously filthy, BR bureaucrats didn't want some throwback to the Victorian age ruining their carefully cultivated modern image. It took another imaginative man with money – Peter Prior, the boss of Bulmers, the Hereford cider company, to change all that. Bulmers persuaded the curators of the national collection to lend them the famous Great Western Railway locomotive *King George V*, which had been lying in an unrestored state in a shed at Swindon since the early 1960s. In 1971 Prior put an advertisement in *The Times* inviting attendance at the ceremony to move the locomotive out of its shed. Cider drinkers were 'especially welcome'. The event was so popular that BR gave in and allowed the newly restored King back on the main line. First of all, steam was restricted to few lines only, but today thoroughbred express engines from all the four pre-grouping companies are allowed to roam over most of the network. Some, such as *Oliver Cromwell*, *Lord Nelson* and *Flying Scotsman,* belong to the nation. Others are owned by syndicates of enthusiasts. The hedge fund manager Jeremy Hosking – No. 333 in the Sunday Times Rich List – owns several, including an A4 class streamliner, *Bittern*, and West Country Class *Braunton*, restored from a scrapyard wreck with the parts of thirteen other scrap locomotives. It is estimated he spent six figures on the restoration. Love, indeed.

Back in 2000 Robertson bought his own steam locomotive – the Southern Railway Merchant Navy Class No. 35005 *Canadian Pacific* – one of the most modern and powerful steam engines ever built. 'You could call it a big boy's toy, and I was exhilarated when I took delivery of it. In fact, as a boy in the 1960s when steam finished I dictated a letter to my mother to send to the general manager of the Southern Region asking how much would it cost to buy one of their Pacifics. So the thought had obviously been at the back of my mind for a long time!' But Robertson got his fingers burnt, literally on one occasion, when the loco blew hot steam back into the cab on a fast Cathedrals Express run to Waterloo, while the head of the Strategic Rail Authority was on the footplate. And a bit like an elderly Jaguar, the locomotive soon needed expensive and uneconomic repairs. It has since been sold to a preserved railway and is unlikely ever to run on the main line again. Robertson wasn't the first to feel the pain. *Flying Scotsman*, the most famous locomotive of all, virtually bankrupted two of its tycoon owners, Alan Pegler and Tony Marchington and severely tested the finances of another rich man, the construction magnate Sir William McAlpine. In the end it had to be rescued by the state in 2004 with a £1.8 million grant from the Heritage Lottery Fund. When the locomotive rolled up at York, National Railway Museum engineers were reportedly shocked by the cost of the further repairs needed.

No such problem with *Oliver Cromwell* this morning, newly restored from the wheels upwards in 2008 and in fine fettle – white wisps of steam floating in a blue sky over the North Downs. The train is running at a canter through the lovely villages of Hollingbourne, Harrietsham, Lenham and Charing, their peace disrupted in recent years not by steam trains but by the roar of the M20 and the high speed rail link to the Channel Tunnel, which run parallel. We don't stop at Ashford, once a famous railway town – the 'Crewe of the Garden of England' as it was once known – though we're passing slowly enough to observe the brand new Javelin bullet trains, whose sleek polished snouts can be seen poking out of the sidings. These 140 mph Japanese-built trains can propel commuters to London's St Pancras in just thirty-seven minutes on Britain's only high speed commuter line.

We swing north over the junction to the Stour Valley line through some of Kent's finest landscapes and historic unspoilt villages. This is the route that Chaucer's pilgrims took – and from the train there is a fine panorama of downland, woodland, orchards, lakes, dykes and marshland. Running through the villages of Wye, Chilham and Chartham, this is as beautiful as any secondary railway in Britain – lucky it was electrified in British Rail's 1955 Modernisation Plan, since this almost certainly saved it from the Beeching axe. But Graeme Bunker, the man in charge of the Cathedrals Express, is less interested in the scenery than whether we're going to get to Canterbury on time. The appropriately-named Bunker is a fully qualified steam fireman, he tells me, 'though you can tell from my newly pressed shirt today that I won't be doing any firing. But I'll be up front with the shovel when the train does a trip to Portsmouth next week.' Bunker is a former high-flying manager from privatised rail who has 'gone native' – he used to be boss of Arriva Trains Wales – but decided to invest his money in ensuring the future of steam, even though at thirty-five he is far too young to remember its heyday. As the writer Brian Hollingsworth points out in *The Pleasures of Railways*, 'There can be few industries which include amongst their staff such a high percentage of people for whom going to work is just another opportunity to indulge their favourite pastime and who go home after nearly every shift secure in the knowledge that they have earned real folding money just by doing what they like doing best.'

'On the face of it,' says Bunker, 'this is the most perfect job in the world – playing trains all day. But there's a lot to do behind the scenes. There's a congested network and you have to get it right, otherwise you end up with a lot of unhappy people. Today we're having a very nice run and we're on time, despite running in with an intensive suburban service.' With his Brunel-like sideburns, you can imagine Bunker back in the mid-nineteenth-century days of railway mania. There is a gleam in his eye as he tells me,

> As far as the other train operators are concerned, it's best that we're invisible. They tolerate us because the running of steam trains like this is enshrined in European legislation. Whether you love or hate steam, they have to accept us – so long as we're safe and pay our bills. Don't worry. We work hard to make sure we remain safe, so the engine is fitted with the latest train protection equipment – modern black box technology comparable with the latest modern trains. And Network Rail, the people who own the tracks, work hard to make us work. What did Peter Parker, the old boss of British Rail say? 'Steam warms the market for the railways in general.'

I had met Bunker a few weeks before, when I had been invited to join a record-breaking run from London to Edinburgh behind

Tornado, a brand new steam locomotive built to the design of the LNER A1 Class Pacifics, probably the most popular modern locomotive type that hadn't had an example preserved. In one of those unlikely stories of true British grit, a group of businessmen had raised £3 million to build it from the 1940s working drawings of its designer Arthur Peppercorn, and Bunker had been appointed the locomotive's operations director. The fact that *Tornado* was simply a reproduction of the real thing seemed not to matter to the thousands of people who lined the trackside, nor to the BBC, who chartered the locomotive to race a vintage Jaguar to the Scottish capital for the *Top Gear* programme with presenter Jeremy Clarkson on the footplate. Regrettably, *Tornado* didn't win, although it would have been a one-way bet if water troughs had still been present on the East Coast Main Line and the loco hadn't needed to stop three times to be topped up, like *Oliver Cromwell* today, from a fire engine at the lineside. Still *Tornado* won a convert from Britain's most famous petrolhead, and the BBC reported that the programme was one of the most successful ever in a show purportedly about cars.

'*Tornado*,' says Bunker, looking dreamily out of the window, 'has made steam cool again. It was really cool in the 1950s, when every boy was a trainspotter, but in the 1980s railway enthusiasts became the butt of jokes – you know, all the stuff about anoraks, halitosis and enamel badges. But we've bridged the gap. If you walk through Cathedrals Express today there are lots of young people who would never have known about steam.' Bunker warms to his theory: 'There are now three tiers of interest in steam as you grow up. For the little ones, it's Thomas the Tank Engine. As kids grow older, it's Harry Potter and the Hogwarts Express, and then through to the *Top Gear* generation. There are three points of access and you can get aboard at any point.' But we have to break off because already, rising silvery through the window on this shimmering summer's day, are the towers of Canterbury cathedral and we are almost at our destination, Canterbury West.

Most of the passengers who disembark here are hotfooting it

for the cathedral, a few pausing to admire the unique Victorian signal box which spans the tracks and to watch *Oliver Cromwell*'s tender being refilled by the local fire brigade. But I notice on the wall by the exit a little plaque announcing that this was once the terminus of the Canterbury and Whitstable Railway, which in 1830 predated the opening of the more famous Liverpool and Manchester as the world's first passenger railway by four months, although much of it was cable-hauled by stationary engines and so disqualifies itself from the premier league. Still, it strikes me that there is a perfect symmetry about arriving at the site of one of the birthplaces of railway passenger travel behind the very last locomotive to haul a normal service passenger train in Britain.

I vaguely recall that *Invicta*, one of the original locomotives of the 'Crab and Winkle', as the Canterbury and Whitstable was known, had been preserved and was on display in a local Canterbury park. 'Dunno where it is, mate,' says the man at the barrier. 'Haven't got a clue. You'll have to ask at the tourist office.' What ignominy for the locomotive that should have been as famous as its sibling the *Rocket*, since both were designed by George Stephenson and emerged from his Newcastle production line at around the same time. *Invicta* has an extra claim to fame as the locomotive that kick-started the preservation movement, having been set aside for posterity in 1844, so legend has it at the instigation of none less than Benjamin Disraeli, who was MP for Maidstone although there is no proof of this story.

But now her fate appears to be obscure, and I have to scour the back streets of the city to find her – wedged into a tiny room of the medieval Hospital for Poor Priests, now the Canterbury Museum. 'You want to see *Invicta,* do you?' says the lady behind the desk, her tone of voice expressing surprise that anyone might have come here, especially to see a bit of old scrap iron. 'Well, I can sell you a Rupert Bear concession for half price.' (Mary Tourtell, the creator of the famous children's cartoon strip, she tells me, was born in the city.) Eventually I find *Invicta*, squashed into a back room next to a Dansette record player and a 1950s washing machine, and it strikes me that she has an uncanny resemblance to Ivor the Engine, whose creator Oliver Postgate was also born in Canterbury. There's a copy of the locomotive's original purchase receipt, written in copperplate, for a surprisingly expensive (by 1830 standards) £635, and a notice that reads, 'The driver stood up on the driving platform for the whole journey – operating the start lever with his left hand, the forward/reverse pedal with his foot and the speed regulator with his right hand.'

Pity I don't study the driving technique more closely, since when I get back to Canterbury West for the next stage of the journey I am ushered up to the footplate of *Oliver Cromwell* to take my place beside the driver for the next thirty-seven miles of the journey to Folkestone. Despite the gap of 120 years, the practical mechanics of steam locomotives scarcely changed between *Invicta* and the Britannia Class, and within a few minutes of the start of this leg of the journey any sentimental views about the great days of steam and why British Railways got rid of the steam locomotive are rapidly dispelled. Not that sharing the footplate with the driver and fireman isn't the thrilling ride of a lifetime. Here is a powerful express locomotive preparing to pull a heavy train up one of the steepest main line gradients in Britain, passing under the white cliffs of Dover through some of the most sensational coastal scenery in the land. But the experience is also a reminder that the sheer filth and physicality of the job would have made it impossible to continue with steam as the era of the train driver as working-class hero drew to a close at the end of the 1960s. The Britannias were the last word in ease of operation – as far as steam locomotives were concerned – with seats for driver and fireman, enclosed cabs, 'self-cleaning' fireboxes and rocking grates that shook the ash down onto the track. Yet they were really no different from the primitive little *Invicta*. If this deafening, sooty, baking-hot monster is state-of the-art, then no wonder crews were clamouring for jobs on unromantic diesels.

But for the people at the lineside and packing the little Kent coast stations this afternoon, it all appears different. I now know what it must have been like to be Princess Diana as crowds wave from the little wayside platforms of Sturry, Minster, Sandwich and Deal, and thousands of shutters snap. 'Keep your head in,' Driver Peter Roberts barks at me, looking every bit like Jean Gabin in Renoir's film *La Bête Humaine*. He and fireman Les Perry have a hundred years of footplate experience between them – true aristocrats of labour, since the skills to drive a steam locomotive in the era of the Eurostar are in very short supply. The sheer brute force needed to feed the firebox means that there are lumps of coal rattling around our feet as Perry humps back-breaking shovel after shovel into the fire while at the same time keeping an eagle eye on the pressure gauge, never letting it drop below 240 pounds per square inch. As we approach the coast, the derelict concrete cooling towers of Richborough power station rear up on the left. During its lifetime it consumed three million tonnes of coal; now it is a poignant mausoleum to the defunct Kent coalfield, shut by Margaret Thatcher in the 1980s. Don't mention it to Arthur Scargill, but the coal being piled at such a rapid rate into *Oliver Cromwell*'s firebox is imported from Russia

'Get some more coal on, and don't let the water drop,' Driver Roberts shouts above the din. 'This next gradient is steeper and longer than Shap.' We're coming up to the notorious Martin Mill gradient outside Dover – with a rise of 1 in 64, tougher than the 1 in 75 on the more famous Shap incline on the West Coast Main Line in Cumbria. The heat from the fire almost skins my eyeballs and the bark of the exhaust is reverberating inside my cranium. 'What was the speed, Pete?' 'We did it at 37 mph.' The eyes of both old men catch each other in triumph.

But if this is steam pushed to the limit, it turns out there is more to come. The route from here through Dover and under the white cliffs into Folkestone is one of the most spectacular pieces of coastal railway engineering in the world. 'It was only seven miles from Dover to Folkestone, but the railway line had the magnificence that all lines do when they run beside the sea,' wrote Paul Theroux in *The Kingdom by the Sea*.

It was not just the sight of the cliffs and the sea breezes. It was also the engineering, all the iron embedded in rock and the inevitable tunnel, the roar of engines and the crashing of waves, the surf just below the tracks, the flecks of salt water on the train windows that faced the sea. The noise was greater because of the cliffs and the light was stranger – land shadows on one side of the train, the luminous sea on the other; and the track was never straight, but always swinging round the bays and coves. It was man's best machine traversing the earth's best feature – the train tracking in the narrow angle between vertical rock and horizontal water.

Could there be any drama greater than this? Well, actually, yes. Charlton and Dover Priory Tunnels don't see steam locomotives very often, and the effect of travelling through them is terrifying. 'Get your head down,' says Driver Roberts as debris from the Victorian tunnel roofs rains down through the open hatch in the cab, blasted off the Victorian brickwork by the exhaust. There is a brief glimpse of the steam of the locomotive projected by the evening sunlight like conversation bubbles over Dover Castle. Driver Roberts keeps up steam through Dover Priory station as more cameras click, then through Harbour Tunnel and the docks, now looking weed-grown and derelict. The port of Dover, the creation of Victorian railway pioneers, has had the guts knocked out of it by its twenty-first-century successor, the Channel Tunnel Link, which begins its descent beneath the sea near the town's old rival Folkestone. Driver Roberts gives a toot on the whistle to the crew of a Polish-registered truck in the car park, as if in sympathy. But neither port is served any longer by glamorous trains such as ours. What a sight we must be to lucky passengers looking back at the coast from the Channel ferries at this moment. It is thirty-eight years since the last Golden Arrow passed through here and into the twin Gothic bores of the 1,387-yard Shakespeare Tunnel. Like the blinded Gloucester in *King Lear*, after whose author the cliff is named, this is high drama in total blackness.

Emerging from the tunnel, there's another poignant moment as we ride high over the back streets of Folkestone, and the line down to the harbour station trails away to the south. Until quite recently heavy boat trains, including the English portion of the Orient Express, would be nudged slowly down the steep gradient so that passengers could embark in comfort directly onto the ships. Now the Eurostars burst at speed from the tunnel along the coast at Cheriton and race through Kent at up to 186 mph. By the time *Oliver Cromwell,* with its slow train, has finished taking on water, courtesy of the local fire brigade, at Folkestone West, the Eurostar set are well on their way to London. But there are special pleasures about travelling at such a leisurely pace as ours. In the kitchen the train's catering supervisor Jackie Bateman and her two chefs are busy preparing a freshly cooked menu of 'Butternut blue cheese and sage tartlet, lemon and rosemary chicken supreme, summer vegetables with creamy vermouth sauce and summer pudding stack with strawberries and clotted cream'. Menus like this are almost extinct on conventional main line trains these days. Once commonplace, railway dining, invented by the Midland Railway in the 1870s, effectively came to an end in 2009, when National Express withdrew its restaurant cars on the King's Cross to Edinburgh line. 'It's a tough business doing freshly cooked meals on a train, especially an old one like this,' says Bateman. 'By the time I've provisioned up the train, overseen the cooking and the washing up and got back to the depot in Southall, west London, it's a twenty-one-hour day.'

Not as long a day, though, as for the locomotive support crew, a bunch of enthusiasts from the 5305 Association, a preservation group subcontracted by the National Railway Museum to maintain and nurse *Oliver Cromwell* who travel with her faithfully wherever she goes. As the train stops briefly at Bromley South before the final leg into Victoria, I am allowed into the holy of holies – the coach behind the engine, whose door is generally locked against the rest of the train. Here is a jumble of greasy overalls, sleeping bags, coffee cups and oil cans, presided over by the chief custodians of

Oliver Cromwell while on tour – a young married couple, let's call them Jane and Justin. 'Please don't print my real name,' says Jane. When I ask why she peers with mock amazement at her breasts inside the bib of her overalls. She's had enough of the media focusing on her just because she's a woman. 'Actually, I'm a qualified steam driver, like Justin. When we're not with *Oliver Cromwell*, we drive passenger trains on the Great Central Railway in Leicestershire. Our home is in Nottinghamshire, but when we're with *Cromwell*, we're in the sleeping bags here.'

It is fashionable to take the jaundiced view that interest in steam on the main line will disappear when Marcus Robertson and his cohort of middle-aged schoolboys passes on. Robertson frowns when I raise this with him. 'Look around you. I can tell you that at least 50 per cent of people on this train haven't the remotest interest in steam. There will always be people who want a nice day out on a train, whether they remember the old days or not.' But maybe this is just nostalgia too. Back in 1952 LT C Rolt, one of the earliest preservationists, wrote, 'A future generation denied the spectacle of an express train in full cry will suffer a loss as great as we have suffered who have never seen a full-rigged ship with all her canvas set.' But who ever sees a fully rigged sailing ship these days? Or cares? Ian Carter in his book *British Railway Enthusiasm*, the first ever academic study of the phenomenon, believes that interest in railways is a passing fad, probably now in its final days. 'British railway enthusiasm is a creature of its time and place, waxing and waning in close relationship to the full-size railway's reputation.' He reckons that ultimately 'the British railway enthusiast's world will vanish like a badly fixed photograph'.

But I wonder. After all the passengers have dispersed, *Oliver Cromwell* reverses out into the twilight at Victoria with a sharp bark and a shower of sparks. The locomotive is now in the care of Justin and Jane and the other young people in the support coach, who are, they have told me, going to 'put her to bed and just make sure she is all right for the night'.

I have a hunch that Carter and the other sceptics may be wrong.

A breath of fresh air: Now rebranded the 'London Overground', the route of the old North London Railway still links the capital's green oases of Hampstead Heath, Kew Gardens and Richmond. Poster, 1870–1913.

CHAPTER SEVEN

THE 08.29 TO RICHMOND –
LONDON'S COUNTRY BRANCH LINE

Stratford to Richmond, via Camden Road
and Willesden Junction

I'm about to take a journey on inner London's only country
railway. Sitting where I am, this may seem a peculiar claim,
since apart from the odd tuft of ragwort and rosebay willowherb
growing between the tracks of Stratford station's Platform 11, I am
in the midst of a concrete-and-glass futuropolis. Over there is the
vast bulk of the new 80,000-seat stadium for London's 2012
Olympics; behind us are the rising towers of the Olympic village.
Not far away, rearing out of the morning mist, are the towers of
Canary Wharf, dominated by César Pelli's No. 1 Canada Square –
the tallest building in the land. Clustered around are its Manhattan-
style neighbours, including Norman Foster's HSBC tower, not quite
so proud since the collapse of Lehman Brothers, whose HQ stands
empty nearby. But with the Olympics in prospect, grimy old
Stratford is in bullish mood. There is the growl of earth movers
everywhere as new blocks of flats sprout up in what was once the
bleakest part of the old industrial East End.

Yet as our little three-coach train rattles down under the Great
Eastern main line and veers westwards past the new Stratford
International station on the fast line to Paris, we are entering a
different world. True, we could hardly be in a more urban setting,
yet the North London Line has more in common with a rural
branch line than any other in the capital. Running in a huge arc for
twenty-two miles around the north of the city, from Stratford to
Richmond, it is the only line to cross the capital without traversing
the centre – although you almost feel that you could reach out and

touch St Pancras station or the BT Tower as you pass by a mile or so away. It was also the only major line within London to be slated for closure by Beeching, who may have confused it with a country railway since for much of the way it passes along the ends of green and leafy back gardens, linking the three oases of Hampstead Heath, Kew Gardens and Richmond along the way. Luckily it escaped the axe, and to this day it remains the most pleasant way to travel from one side of the hurried metropolis to the other.

Like a proper country railway too, the North London demonstrates that the greatest metropolis in the world is little more than a series of villages. They may jostle together geographically in an urban melee, but socially and culturally they are often a million miles apart. In the sixty-two minutes it will take our train to trundle from Stratford to Richmond we will pass from neighbourhoods where newcomers from Albania to Zaire eke out a life in slums that would have been familiar to Mayhew or Booth, to the Islington heartland of City bankers with their multi-million-pound Georgian villas and on to the posh suburbs of Kew and Richmond.

Originally, the directors of the North London Railway didn't care much about people at all. Projected in 1850 to carry goods from Birmingham and the great manufacturing cities of the north to the London Docks, it branched off the Euston main line at Primrose Hill, meandering eastwards through north London till it bumped into the Thames at Poplar. But as the city expanded on its northern heights, there was a lucrative new market for a hitherto undiscovered species – the suburban commuter. The line was soon extended through the 'two up, two down' west London suburbs, as John Betjeman called them, crossing the Thames to posh Richmond. An army of clerks thronged the new line, and to cater for them, a large and handsome terminus was built next to Liverpool Street in the Lombardic style by the company's engineer, William Baker. So splendid was the new Broad Street station, with its ornate roofs and chimney stacks and ironwork, it made the Great Eastern's huge terminus appear very modest indeed. The little NLR had hit the big time. As the *Railway News* commented at the time, 'The history of the North London is … a curious one and if a railway be a sensitive thing it must feel as much astonished at being brought into Broad Street as Christopher Sly, the tinker felt when he found himself metamorphosed into a duke.'

Until the coming of the Tube, the North London was the biggest suburban railway north of the Thames. But in the 1950s it went into a long slow decline. After decades of being allowed to moulder, Broad Street was demolished in 1985 and is now interred under the hideous corporate red marble of the Broadgate office block. The North London was diverted to Stratford and now runs into no central London terminus, but this little railway has always been a fighter, and after many scrapes with oblivion and rebrandings, has finally joined the Tube system with a grand new title – the London Overground – and an extension along the course of the East London Tube Line to Crystal Palace, West Croydon and other stations south of the Thames.

'Did you know it's always been faster to travel across London on our line than on the District Line of the Tube?' Grace, the guard, tells me. (The NLR was a rarity on urban railways until recently in still having guards – although they are being eliminated as new more sophisticated trains and signalling are introduced.) Grace, whose parents came to London from Nigeria, has been with the line for nine years, through its previous brandings as the North London Link and the absurdly named Silverlink ('Always sounded like my auntie's tea service,' she says). Now Grace is particularly pleased with her smart new jerkin in the grey and orange house colours of the Tube. She proudly displays the embroidered London Transport roundel, a badge of permanence if ever there was one.

My train from Stratford arrives at the first westbound station, Hackney Wick, in minutes – not because we have gathered speed but because all the stations are so close and this slowest of slow trains rarely gets above 20 mph at any point on the journey. This is the heart of Hackney – rustbowl London, a wasteland of derelict factories and streets that appear to go nowhere. Iain Sinclair, the chronicler of unconventional London life, describes it thus in his book about Hackney, *That Rose-Red Empire*: 'A once Arcadian suburb of grand houses, orchards and conservatories, Hackney declined into a zone of asylums, hospitals and dirty industry. Persistently revived, reinvented, betrayed, it has become a symbol of inner-city chaos, crime and poverty.' But it also represents the vibrancy of ethnic London at its best. By Homerton the carriage is buzzing with what seem to be most of the 150 languages that are currently spoken in the metropolis.

Sadly, at this end of the line the magnificent station buildings of the North London Railway, designed by E H Horne in the Venetian-Gothic style and constructed of white Suffolk brick, Portland stone and terracotta, have mostly gone. By the end of the 1950s, the infrastructure of the old North London was like something from a Gothic horror movie. Water dripped through ceilings, algae ate away at elegant carvings, slates dropped from roofs and once-splendid wooden structures mouldered away with dry rot. Weeds grew through cracks in the platforms. It was the perfect scenario for the Beeching axe. But change was in the air. There were the first inklings that the endless advance of the motor car might end up strangling London, and local authorities along the line roused themselves to save it from closure. Jo Grimond, leader of the Liberal Party, wrote an article in the *Manchester Guardian* suggesting that it should be incorporated in the Tube map, a status it has only recently fully achieved, nearly half a century later. But when the North London was finally reprieved in 1965 by the Labour transport minister Tom Fraser, British Railways had their revenge and butchered nearly all the heritage – substituting bus shelters and huts built from the cheapest materials where Horne's commodious buildings had once stood. One of the most monstrous acts of vandalism was the total demolition of Dalston Junction, once a grand station with several platforms, where even in the early 1960s passengers might find a roaring coal fire in the waiting room on a winter's night. You could once, in the heyday of the line, pick up a restaurant-car express to Wolverhampton from here. But as it sank into decline, passengers might be forgiven for thinking they had alighted at a ghost station. What a pity, since a new but more spartan Dalston Junction has opened as part of the new route taking the North London Line south of the Thames through the world's first underwater tunnel, designed by Marc Brunel, Isambard Kingdom's father, at Rotherhithe.

Sadly though we shall never again be able to take the slow train to Broad Street. Which is why I am abandoning the train at Dalston Kingsland and taking a rare bus diversion from my journey. This morning I am on a special mission to rediscover memories of Broad Street, because my father was among the hundreds of thousands of Mr Pooters who commuted into the station every day, making the fortunes of the North London Railway and its successor, the London and North Western Railway. (Henry Pooter, hero of George and Weedon Grossmith's novel *The Diary of a Nobody*, makes no mention of the North London Railway, although it is a fair bet that he would have used its services to travel from his home in Holloway to his job as a clerk, like my father, in the City.)

This is a social world that has almost entirely vanished. For forty years, Stanley Williams caught the 8.23 each morning from West End Lane station (now West Hampstead) to his job as a clerk in the offices of the Royal London Insurance Company in Finsbury Square. Not only did the timing of the trains not change much, nor did people's jobs. These days, according to the latest statistics, the average twenty-something stays in a job for less than two years. Stanley Williams stayed loyal to the North London until his retirement, always preferring the style and comfort of its electric trains to the Tube. The line was electrified as long ago as 1916, and one of the original cars, which lasted in service until the 1960s, is in the National Railway Museum in York – the oldest electric multiple unit in the land. No wonder it lasted so long, since its equipment was supplied by one of the best engineering firms in

Switzerland – Oerlikon Maschinenfabrik of Zurich. Even in the bleakest days of the nationalised railway in the 1960s the North London continued the tradition of having trains specially designed for it, although the Class 501 units, built in British Railways' works in the 1950s, did not have such splendidly comfortable cushions as the Oerlikons, nor did they have the leather straps to open the carriage windows, which were a favourite trophy for local schoolboys and their penknives.

Dalston Kingsland is a mean and shabby station built at the end of 1973 after Dalston Junction was closed and passenger services diverted to Stratford. Possibly the only sign of the universe Mr Pooter or my father once inhabited is the Railway Tavern next to the station, on old Irish boozer covered in puke-coloured tiles, which still has its traditional pub sign, with a picture of a train looking more like the red engine in Graham Greene's *The Little Train* than anything the North London Railway might have run. In the bar, where there is a framed front page of the *News Chronicle* announcing 'Crowning Glory – Everest is Climbed' along with the words of the Irish national anthem, elderly West Indians in baseball caps slumber over halves of Red Stripe. 'We don't serve food here,' says Rose the landlady as she pours a Guinness in the way only the Irish do, and directs me to Ridley Road market over the road, which is as potent a distillation of multicultural urban life as can be found anywhere on the planet. Amid hundreds of stalls selling every conceivable foodstuff from cows' feet to parrotfish, old-fashioned cockney stallholders with fat jewellery jostle with ringletted Rastas and toothless elderly men speaking Urdu doing deals over boxes of mangoes and yams. There is every kind of tripe, stomach and testicle here – heaving innards of all kinds dripping blood and who knows what other fluids. It is said that with a quiet word at the back of a stall you could negotiate, if you so wished, for some black-market monkey steaks here, but I settle for a relatively conservative goat curry, sneaking into the back of a huge Victorian church to eat it surreptitiously. ST MARK'S, DALSTON, CATHEDRAL OF THE EAST END, says the board outside. It is apparently the only church in Europe with a working barometer, but when I try to put some money in the offertory box, I find it has been crowbarred out of the wall. 'It's OK. Give it to me,' says a wizened man emerging from the darkness. I reckon not.

I wonder what the stonemasons of Dove Brothers, Islington, the builders of St Mark's, might have thought. Almost certainly they would have made their way to work here on the North London Railway. But for me it is the No. 242 bus (Homerton Hospital to Liverpool Street) south along the Kingsland Road to the site of what John Betjeman once called the 'saddest of London stations'. As a small boy travelling to the City with my father – doing overtime to support a young family on a Saturday morning – I recall vividly Broad Street's deserted air of faded glory. Betjeman wrote evocatively, 'In the sixties, the magnificent iron roof over the train shed was removed. The large Lombardic buffet and the shops for city clerks were shut down and in 1970 the scale-model 4-4-0 engine whose wheels went round if you put a penny in the slot was either removed or stolen.'

Sad, because I invested what seemed an enormous amount of my pocket money standing on tiptoes watching the wheels revolve. This little engine, which whizzed away without going anywhere, and the Italian man in the buffet who would tip a sugar shaker into my dandelion and burdock drink to create a volcano of fizz, were, for some inexplicable reason, some of the most profound memories of my boyhood. Betjeman went on (writing in 1972):

> Standing in the empty concourse at Broad Street today, one has a feeling of its former greatness. A few steps back will take you into what was once an enormous booking hall whose timber roof towers above the station shops. Along on the concourse now stands the 1914 war memorial of the North London, a miniature version of the Cenotaph in Whitehall . . . May God Save the Old North London!

Of course he didn't. At least, not in that joyous incarnation of Betjeman's time. Sitting in Starbucks in the Broadgate Circle amid the 1980s corporate pink granite over a large macchiato, I reckon the grid reference is about right for the booking office, if not my little penny-in-the-slot engine. Just fancy – at the turn of the century there were more arrivals at Broad Street than at Euston and Paddingon combined. It was the Edwardian equivalent of London City Airport, with frock-coated City gents preferring to take trains to the Midlands from here, complete with the services of a travelling typist provided by the railway. Only Liverpool Street and Victoria had more trains. But not a brick or a shard remains of Broad Street, not even the echo of a whistle. Certainly not a memory. I ask Alphonse, the 'barista', if he knows there was once a great railway station here. 'Maybe like the Gare D'Orsay?' he ventures. Yes. But unlike the Parisians, Londoners didn't bother to save it.

Still, not all is lost. Small railway companies like the North London were often grand in disproportion to their size, and despite the wreckers of the 1960s a few mini-Broad Streets have survived. I take the No. 48 bus to pick up the line again at Hackney Central, where more than sixty years since it closed the station building is almost intact, although now it is a Turkish restaurant. Squint a bit, and its palazzo-like frontage with its Gothic pilasters could just about be perched on the bank of the Grand Canal.

But there are other ghosts that haunt this stretch of line as it runs through Hackney. Do the local estate agents and bank staff, polishing off the last of their kebabs this late lunchtime, know anything about the grisly events of 1864? On Saturday 9 July that year Thomas Briggs, chief clerk at Messrs Robards and Co. of Lombard Street in the City of London, caught the 9.50 p.m. train from Fenchurch Street to his home at 5 Clapton Square in Hackney. Later in the journey, two clerks, by coincidence at the same bank, who had purchased tickets for Highbury, opened the door of a first-class compartment and found something wet on the cushions – blood. It was everywhere – on the walls, on the windows, on the ceiling of the compartment. Later that evening Alfred Ekin, the driver of a train heading back to Fenchurch Street, found

Thomas Briggs severely injured on the track. He had been bludgeoned with a blunt instrument and died soon afterwards.

The murder made history, as it was the first ever to take place on a British train. Astonishing really, since it was thirty-four years since the opening of the Liverpool and Manchester Railway, the first fully-fledged passenger line – and what opportunities there were for thieves and robbers in the gaslit and often-lawless world of mid-Victorian Britain. The Briggs murder was sensational in other ways too. The murderer, a young German called Franz Muller, was quickly traced through the distinctive design of his hat, which he had left behind in the compartment during the kerfuffle. By this time he had fled to New York on the sailing ship *Victoria*. But the world of transportation was changing, and not just on the railways. Detectives jumped on a steamship, the *City of Manchester,* and after a thrilling race across the Atlantic were waiting on the quayside to arrest Muller. He was tried, found guilty and, despite his plea of innocence and an appeal to Queen Victoria from Prince Wilhelm I of Prussia, publicly hanged in Newgate prison. The case had far-reaching consequences. A public outcry led to the end of public hangings, and the new electric trains of the North London Railway were designed with long open saloons rather than the more risky single compartments. Muller's name lived on in the description of a particular kind of black beaver hat.

After this an air of murder seemed to hang about the old North London, which was the scene for two more nationally famous killings. On 9 January 1900, Louise Masset became the first woman to be hanged in the twentieth century. She had been convicted of killing her three-and-a-half-year-old son Manfred and dumping his body in the ladies' lavatory at Dalston Junction. Curiously, fourteen years later to the day the body of another child was found on the line, this time under the seat on the 4.14 p.m. from Chalk Farm. In a celebrated case, his father was charged with the murder but acquitted. He became a newspaper seller on Liverpool Street station, where he was killed in an air raid in 1941.

But enough of this gruesome stuff. It is time for one of the finest free shows available from any railway carriage in the land, best enjoyed between dusk falling and the closing of curtains on, say, a November evening. For between Hackney Central and Richmond the line runs intimately cheek by jowl with the living rooms and kitchens of the houses along the line. Glimpsed through the trees at the end of a back garden or spotted from the vantage point of the many viaducts that run for miles above the rooftops it is possible to get an anthropologist's-eye view of the entire social spectrum of the metropolis. Here is a mother making tea for her children freshly home from school. There is a writer seemingly lost for words staring up from his desk, the train a welcome diversion from more pressing things. Now a clinch between two lovers, caught for just a brief moment and then gone. As we clatter into Camden Road we are in the territory of John Betjeman's 'Business Girls'.

> From the geyser ventilators
> Autumn winds are blowing down
> On a thousand business women
> Having baths in Camden Town
>
> Waste pipes chuckle into runnels,
> Steam's escaping here and there,
> Morning trains through Camden cutting
> Shake the Crescent and the Square.
>
> Early nip of changeful autumn,
> Dahlias glimpsed through garden doors,
> At the back precarious bathrooms
> Jutting out from upper floors

Betjeman, who grew up in nearby Highgate, loved the North London, recalling that 'the earliest sounds I can remember are the chuffs of its 4-4-0 engines coming up from Kentish Town to Gospel Oak'. He would certainly have approved of the transformation of Camden Road station, relatively intact and with new paintwork gleaming. It is the only one of Horne's original stations to survive in railway use and still sports its original name CAMDEN TOWN STATION engraved in stone along the roofline. (It was renamed Camden Road in the 1950s.) Shame the period effect is rather ruined by the rather gaudy London Overground corporate colour scheme. Just before it enters the station, the train crosses the main lines from King's Cross and then St Pancras, and through the window is a fine panorama of the central London skyscape. The futuristic-looking tube over the tracks is the entrance to the twin bores of the Channel Tunnel Link, which runs underground for twelve miles, to re-emerge down the line on the east London fringes at Dagenham.

Soon the junction with the Euston main line branches away to the left, snaking over the top of Camden Market, now the fourth most visited tourist attraction in London. Brace yourself for the whiff of frying onions and patchouli oil, and it feels you could almost touch the chimney pots of the Hawley Arms, an old boozer famed as a temple to the indie bands of the Seventies but latterly the hangout of the singer Amy Winehouse and the model Kate Moss. To the left is the Roundhouse, the former engine shed of the London and Birmingham Railway in the days when the trains had to be hauled by cable up the incline from Euston. After many changes of fortune, the future of the Grade I-listed building, now an arts centre, is secure after undergoing a £26 million refurbishment. Sadly the same cannot be said of the splendid Victorian ironwork of the neighbouring Primrose Hill station, smashed down secretly by Network Rail one night at the end of 2007 after local activists had tried to get it reopened. The heavy freights that traverse the junction at this point from the industrial cities of the north are no longer destined for the London Docks, now long gone. Nor do they bear the names of proud Victorian industrialists, exporting to the empire from the 'workshop of the world'. Instead the traffic flow is mostly the other way – imported through the docks at Felixstowe. The names of oriental shipping firms such as China Lines and Cosco on the long trains of container wagons tell of how much the world has turned.

This is an area rich in railway firsts. Robert Stephenson's London and Birmingham was the first main line out of London and the reason for the North London's birth. Turning west over the Hampstead Junction Railway towards Kentish Town, we pass the site of Kentish Town signal cabin, where in 1860 engineers installed a marvellous piece of equipment – the world's first interlocking signalling device, which physically prevented conflicting train movements happening at the same time, effectively stopping trains bumping into one another. The little North London had already been the first railway to establish everyday use of the continuous brake on its carriages in 1855 and the first to use coal gas to light its trains. In 1900 it became the first to install automatic ticket machines.

While in the world of superlatives it's worth noting that the Kentish Town Viaduct, which we are crossing now, has ninety-four arches. Good news for car breakers, but less so for inhabitants of the bedrooms of the houses in the little terraced houses that cluster round. Noise and vibration may be one thing, but dozens of prying eyes as you roll out of bed in the morning are quite another. Visible from here too are the spires of the many churches that came to minister to the huddled working classes of the narrow streets – St Martin's, St Luke's, St Silas's. This was a neighbourhood renowned for its rogues and villains in Victorian times and is not much different now, according to one of the local vicars, who I know well. In an attempt to bring the population nearer to God, the directors of the North London operated a strict rule that no trains should run during 'church time' on Sunday mornings. This meant all trains being halted for around two hours, a practice greatly approved of by railwaymen, but not sadly on spiritual grounds. NLR staff rarely went to church themselves but took the opportunity for a rare decent lunch in what was often a sixteen-hour working day. John Betjeman recalls that the general manager of the line refused to allow WH Smith's bookstalls on the line to sell any papers which he considered vulgar.

Now we are truly in a bucolic world as the train rolls past the green acres of Hampstead Heath, with a fine view of Parliament Hill on the right. The latter gets its name from Civil War days, when it was occupied by troops loyal to Parliament, although nowadays it is better known as a favourite spot for children to launch their kites on a breezy day. The ambience is still green as we pass rows of allotments, where you might catch sight of a famous Hampstead author or two tending a row of runner beans or rigging up a scarecrow. Waiting lists for allotments in this most upmarket area of north London are among the longest in Britain at forty years, so don't set your heart on one. At Hampstead Heath station the sign reads, 'Alight here for the Royal Free Hospital' – perhaps unfortunate since on Easter Monday 1892 the station was the scene of a terrible accident. Then as now, ''Appy 'Ampstead' was the playground of north London, especially popular on bank holidays, when tens of thousands came to ride the donkeys or take a spin on the roundabouts. But at 5 p.m. on that fateful day the sky grew overcast and the crowds headed for home. As they packed onto the footbridge heading to the platforms, it collapsed under the weight, killing six children and two women, as well as inflicting terrible injuries on others.

Even on the hottest of summer days there is a chill as the train enters the tunnel here, though it may have less to do with malign events than the fact that it runs at a great depth, 160 feet under the heights of Hampstead. Even though fourteen million of the finest Staffordshire bricks were used to line it, the London clay above is constantly shifting – the tunnel collapsed during its construction in 1858 and has needed constant remedial work ever since. The train emerges from the darkness at Finchley Road and Frognal, a lovely name gracing what must be one of the ugliest stations on the line, with a prefabricated booking office and bus shelters on the platform festooned with razor wire – an environment acknowledged by the local graffiti artists, who have had a spree here – although minus the talent of Banksy.

Nostalgia impels me to get off at West Hampstead because this is the stop from where my father caught the train to Broad Street every day without fail for his marathon in the City. It was called West End Lane then, named after the little hamlet along the road. I can dimly remember the place myself. The hiss of gas lamps, the buildings sooty and dilapidated after the war. But it had a proper staff of three in those days – a booking clerk, a roly-poly porter with an uncanny resemblance to the comedian Peter Kay and a ticket collector called Cyril. Cyril had a limp because he had been tortured by the Japanese in the war (something beyond my youthful comprehension). But I remember the peak of his hat was always well polished, and every morning in winter Cyril always lit a roaring fire in the waiting room. No waiting room here today – just another prefabricated bus shelter, littered with McDonald's wrappers.

The train rolls on – over the Kilburn High Road at Brondesbury, through Brondesbury and Brondesbury Park – prosperous with well-heeled BBC executives in spacious Edwardian houses – past the car breakers and scrapyards of Kensal Rise and Willesden Junction. Here is the site of the Old Oak Common engine sheds, where the King and Castle Class locos for the crack expresses from Paddington were once housed, and small boys crept in with their Ian Allan spotters' books, only to get a clip round the ear from the shedmaster if they were caught.

I take a break at Acton Central, where Ibrahim, the station supervisor, is whistling cheerfully to himself. Maybe it's something to do with the fact that the station has retained its Victorian country atmosphere, complete with level crossing at the end of the platform. Or maybe because Transport for London has installed new electronic barriers, which means he no longer has to deal with the fare dodgers that were long the bane of the line. Ibrahim is especially proud of the little home-made tableau of the history of the line on the westbound platform, composed of old black-and-white photos stuck onto card. Here is the station building as it was long ago, in much leafier surroundings. Next to it is a picture of one of the elegant little 4-4-0 tanks with a rake of carriages. 'Built to last for ever they were. All made in the company's own works at Bow,' he tells me. Ibrahim is clearly a buff and warms to his theme: 'And the carriages, all made of teak, with red and blue cushions. Very unusual they were because they only had four wheels, like cattle trucks.'

But now the level crossing gates are closing and I dash across to the other platform for the next train. We really are out of town now, stopping at Kew Gardens station, built in the London and South Western Railway style, with cherry trees on the platforms, and indistinguishable from many of that company's stations in farthest Devon and Cornwall. There is a perfect little station buffet here, although access is no longer available from the platform since the Mayor of London's diktat that alcohol shall not be drunk on London stations.

We are now sandwiched between the red, white and blue trains of the District Line for the final gallop into Richmond. The North London appears a bit of an interloper in this station, built in the breezy seaside art deco style of the Southern Railway. Appropriate in its own way, since we are only a few hundred yards from the sunny banks of the Thames – not the dark grungy river we left behind in east London, but a much more cheerful-looking Thames that rolls sweetly down from Oxford, fitting for the end of the line on London's country railway.

But the journey didn't quite end here. A few weeks later I was in the York National Railway Museum at closing time. This is the nicest part of the day at the museum, since with most of the visitors gone home it is possible to summon the shades of the great steam locomotives which inhabit it. They may be dead and lifeless now, but with the dusk falling it is possible to imagine them as they were once – fast and furious with fire in their bellies. And there it is in the twilight. The little 4-4-0 from my childhood, still in its glass case and still working – though now you have to insert a 10p coin to get the wheels turning. Sir John Betjeman, who so loved the North London, believed it was lost. Would he have died a happier man, I wonder, if he had known that it was found?

My heart's in the Highlands: 'Standard Class 5' No. 73078 and ex-LMS 'Black Five' No. 44976 take water at Crianlarich with the 2.56 p.m. restaurant car train from Fort William to Glasgow in May 1959.

CHAPTER EIGHT

THE 21.15 FROM EUSTON — THE 'DEERSTALKER EXPRESS' TO THE REMOTEST STATION IN BRITAIN

London Euston to Mallaig, via Edinburgh, Glasgow, Crianlarich, Rannoch and Fort William

There are few more unlovely gateways to a long-distance railway journey in the world than Euston station in London. 'Even by the bleak standards of Sixties architecture,' wrote one correspondent in *The Times* in 2007,

> Euston is one of the nastiest concrete boxes in London:
> devoid of any decorative merit; seemingly concocted to
> induce maximum angst among passengers; and a blight on
> surrounding streets. The design should never have left the
> drawing board – if, indeed, it was ever on a drawing
> board. It gives the impression of having been scribbled on
> the back of a soiled paper bag by a thuggish android with a
> grudge against humanity and a vampiric loathing of
> sunlight.

The contrast today with what was once here could not be starker. Nowadays the only monuments travellers will find where the famous old Euston once stood are the temples to the global empires of fast food – Burger King, Harry Ramsden's and Café Ritazza. But here, just by the ticket collector on Platform 9, once towered the huge, soot-stained and romantically majestic emblem of Britain's mighty Railway age. Built by Philip Hardwick in 1837, it was inspired by the Doric propylaeum at the top of the Acropolis in Athens and built to celebrate the arrival of Robert

Stephenson's London and Birmingham Railway from the north. It was the largest Doric propylaeum ever built and reached a height of more than seventy feet. The fact that it was widely judged the most significant monument of the Railway Age did nothing to save it, and despite a campaign by John Betjeman and other architectural worthies its death warrant was signed by Prime Minister Harold Macmillan in 1961 to a chorus of public outrage. At the end of 2009, as the credit crunch set back plans to demolish Euston and start again, millions were spent tarting the station up, although the twenty-nine million passengers who use the station every year may fail to notice the difference.

But all is not lost. Even in the modern Euston it is possible for determined souls to summon up some of the glamour and romance that rightfully belongs here. Sneak past the Square Pie shop and the Bangers Bros sausage takeaway, and turn left at the statue of poor old Robert Stephenson, the only surviving remnant from the booking hall of the old station, now marooned beneath the black glass and concrete Network Rail HQ – a handy toilet for pigeons and a repository for discarded coffee cups. Just by the bus station is a pub called the Doric Arch, unexceptional in itself, but at the top of the stairs to the bar is a poster which I've always regarded as one of the most evocative to be found of any railway station in London.

It has no date but clearly derives from Edwardian times. In the picture it is mid-evening on the Euston Road and the gilded capital letters spelling EUSTON at the top of the arch positively gleam with the reflected light as dusk falls. A parade of early open-top motor cars and horse-drawn carriages, with their tail lights winking, progresses towards the arch, where between the great Doric columns a golden light beckons. 'London and North Western Railway,' the legend declares. 'Sleeping car saloons with every modern convenience are attached to the night trains from Euston.'

Ah, the thrill of a lost era, you might say. But you'd be wrong.

Even a century later and in the age of the high speed train, sleeping cars still depart on night trains from Euston. After the last of the commuters have scurried back to Herts and Bucks suburbia and the concourse vendors are packing away their stalls, you will find a palpable sense of expectation around Platform 15 where the 'Deerstalker Express' departs nightly (Saturdays excepted) for its 520-mile journey to Fort William in the West Highlands. This is not the real name of the 21.15 departure of course, since no train out of Euston these days has a name, and the titles of the great Anglo-Scottish trains of the past – the Night Scotsman, the Royal Scot and the Caledonian – have long vanished into distant memory. But it might as well be, since if any service in Britain oozes the glamour and romance of the great trains of the past, then this is it. Sixteen coaches, and at the front is the powerful 110-mph electric Class 90 locomotive No. 90 021 – the last class of express locomotives built at the famous Crewe works, ending a British engine-building tradition of 150 years. Indeed, you will be very lucky to find any passenger train on the British national network still hauled by a locomotive in the old-fashioned sense, even though this one, despite bearing the branding *Caledonian Sleeper*, is actually the property of a subsidiary of the German state railway in one of those quirks of rail privatisation that it is best not to enquire into too deeply unless you are a groupie of the Office of Rail Regulation.

There is no train in Britain that goes farther and offers more pampering to its passengers than this one – splitting off into three separate sections at Edinburgh Waverley, with sleeping coaches peeling away to Aberdeen, Inverness and Fort William, where the last of the passengers will arrive more than twelve hours from now. You can almost feel the train puffed up with importance in the platform. Will you be installed in a berth next to a Scottish laird returning from his London club to the family estate? Or a Scots MSP heading back for a crucial vote at Holyrood? Perhaps an Edinburgh banker or two rushing home to deal with a credit crisis? More mundanely, your fellow passenger could be a hitch-hiker on a budget with one of the train's famously cheap Internet tickets.

Who knows? But here is Abdul my sleeping car steward, a tall man with an immaculately trimmed beard, to greet me, standing to attention with a clipboard. 'What would you like for breakfast, sir?' he asks, scouring his printed list for my name. 'The Bacon Roll or the Continental?' One of the advertising slogans for this train is that it is 'a little bit of Scotland come to London'. Abdul, who lives in Edinburgh, tells me that many Scots enjoy bacon rolls, but he has never eaten one himself, nor would he be likely to. Another cultural twist of the times prescribes that sleeping car attendants such as Abdul should be known as 'hosts' (much blander-sounding than 'stewards', although Abdul is far too professional to comment). But otherwise very little has changed from when the cultural historian Roger Lloyd wrote about the pleasures of night trains in 1952,

> Practically every sleeping car passenger approaches the
> train and clutches his special tickets with a real thrill.
> There is the attendant who quickly identifies and welcomes
> his guests, addressing them both by name and title. It may
> no doubt be very childish, and even a trifle snobbish, to be
> pleased when greeted by name, but it does undoubtedly
> light a little glow inside not to be treated as just an
> anonymous member of the travelling public. Down a
> deeply padded and soft-footed corridor, the attendant takes
> you to your own tiny cabin and you think – this time with
> an anti-social satisfaction – that it cannot matter to you
> how crowded the train is since this kingdom is for that
> night your very own, and nobody else can get into it.

There is air-conditioning now, though modern passengers might grumble about having to pad down the corridor in the night for the toilet, and potentially having to share with a stranger if they hold a standard-class ticket. Conversely, the intimate size of the compartments has historically attracted people in search of romantic liaisons – a friend of mine, the editor of a national newspaper, carried on an extramarital affair for years in a railway sleeping car. It was the perfect hideaway and an unsurpassable alibi.

But now the whistle is blowing and we are about to head off into the night. Goodbye to the thunder of traffic on the Euston Road. Tomorrow, breakfast will be served with wheels clacking across as remote a track as it is possible to find within Great Britain, where, if you are lucky, you will be greeted by a curious stag pressing its hot breath against the window to see what's on the menu. This is one of the world's great journeys at any time of the year, but for maximum effect it is best taken on midsummer's night when daylight is longest. Once, in the days when the London and North Western Railway operated the line, you might have found a Precursor Class locomotive named after Shakespeare's Oberon on this train (the LNWR was fond of classical names), but tonight we must be satisfied with the magic of the views as we race the setting sun on history's most magnificently engineered railway tracks. Our journey will take us on the metals of Robert Stephenson's London and Birmingham and Grand Junction Railways, awakening in the suburbs of Glasgow in the morning to see the full glory of the West Highland line – itself a 164-mile journey along a winding single track through the most desolately beautiful railway in Europe.

Another special reason to take the Deerstalker Express is that this, and its sister sleeper, the Lowland Express to Glasgow and Edinburgh, are the only trains of the day to progress at a sedate enough pace properly to appreciate the views from the main line north out of Euston. Richard Branson's 125-mph Pendolinos, which operate the day service to Glasgow, are the sleekest of greyhounds, operating the most intensive inter-city service in the world, with three trains an hour to Manchester and three to

Birmingham. Running at speeds of 125 mph has many virtues, but window gazing is not among them. So make the most of it, and settle back in the lounge car, which is one of those comfy seventies carriages you thought had disappeared, with a nightcap at your elbow. (The night services to Scotland can claim the only leather sofas on a British train, and unlike those notorious buffets that always seem to close at Reading or Stevenage will serve until the last passenger has gone to bed.)

No. 90 021 makes light work of the gradient out of Euston, despite the 21.15 being the heaviest train in regular service in Britain. It is hard to imagine that when Robert Stephenson's London and Birmingham Railway was opened in 1838 the incline was so daunting that the trains had to be hauled up by cable. They were then taken onwards by little locos housed in the Chalk Farm Round-house, now the legendary arts venue, which can be seen clearly from the window on the right. Next door, where a huge Morrison's supermarket now stands, is the site of the great engine house that operated the cables – as emblematic of the Victorian era as the super-market chains are of our own. Still, the line is as flat as can be for the next hundred miles, and is one of the greatest engineering achieve-ments of the Victorian era. Built in just five years by 20,000 men, the feat was calculated to have been more labour intensive than even the construction of the Great Pyramid at Giza.

The London suburbs pass by in a flash, with the spire of Harrow church towering on the hill on the left, burial place of Thomas Port, who had the unfortunate distinction of being the first crewman in the world to be killed. He fell between two carriages and his legs were severed. Scarcely before the drinks have arrived, we are at Watford Junction. Two schoolboys at the end of the platform scribble our numbers in a spotters' book. Yes, spotters' guides are still published even in the era of Facebook and the Nintendo Wii, although spotters themselves are as rare as locomotives on passenger trains these days. What a shame our Class 90 doesn't have a red and silver headboard on the front, as it might have had in the 1950s. But no time for regrets as we gather speed into the Chiltern Hills, through the vast cutting at Tring, running parallel to those other great highways to the north: William Jessop's Grand Union Canal and Ernest Marples' M1, now half a century old. (Little boys and grown-up little boys never fail to thrill at the way even slower trains like ours overtake all those BMWs and Mercs stuck at 70 mph in the fast lane.) But despite all the bustle, there are still lonely spots.

Near here, at lonely Sears Crossing in Buckinghamshire, the Great Train Robbers halted the Glasgow to Euston 'postal'. The heist – on 8 August 1963 – couldn't have been simpler. Buster Edwards, Ronnie Biggs and their chums placed a glove over the green signal and wired up a red light with a battery. The robbers got away with £2.6 million in used banknotes (worth around £50 million in 2009). The money was never found. Couldn't happen now. There are simply too many trains passing by for a stopped train not to be spotted. What I do spy, as we pass through Wolverton, are the gleaming burgundy Class 67 locomotives of the royal train, manoeuvring Her Majesty's coaches out of the shed where they are stored. It is a reminder of what good friends the royal family have been to the railways since Queen Victoria became the first reigning monarch to travel by train in 1842, describing the experience as 'quite charming'. Somewhere in the kingdom tomorrow people will be getting out the bunting for the arrival of the Queen – or most likely the Prince of Wales, who has a sentimental fondness for the train, since it was reputed to have been a much-used location during his 'courting days'.

We plunge into the notorious Kilsby Tunnel, one mile and 666 yards long. Robert Stephenson, who had mastered the steam engine and the opposition of English landlords to his projects, was nearly mastered himself by Kilsby Tunnel. The great engineer encountered quicksands 120 feet below ground, which turned the tunnel into an underground lake. Experts told him to abandon it. But, Moses-like, he turned back the waters by designing a pumping engine, which he ran for eight months till it was dry. Just to prove it still is, watch out for the shaft of light from above ground midway through, which is depicted in a famous and much-reprinted engraving made in 1837 by John Cooke Bourne. The light from above used to offer great solace to tunnel-shy ladies, who protected their modesty by carrying candles to augment the dim gas lamps in the carriage roof.

Not much is left of Stephenson's original architecture of the line, swept away in the £9 billion upgrade completed by Network Rail in 2009. We race through the rebuilt Rugby station, where Thomas Arnold, the Victorian head of Rugby School, stood on a bridge to watch a train go by and declared, 'I rejoice to see it and declare that feudality is gone for ever.' The board of First Group, which runs this train and is arguably the most successful of the privatised rail firms, would obviously agree. Rugby's old steel and glass overall roof – familiar to Dickens and reinvented by him at 'Mugby Junction' – has been sacrificed to the modernisers. Tamworth and Stafford, farther down the line, have been shamelessly and inelegantly modernised too. Much of the new lineside infrastructure, sadly, looks like the architecture of the old East Germany. English Heritage has saved the charming Jacobean-style buildings of Atherstone, the ancient capital of the hatting industry. But the red-brick stationmaster's house designed by J W Livock is boarded up without a current use – a rather poignant contrast to the vast lorry depot of the logistics firm TNT next door.

There are many other curiosities to be spied from the window in this rural heart of England. Just before Norton Bridge in Staffordshire is Izaak Walton's cottage, where the patron saint of fishermen wrote *The Compleat Angler*. It is so close to the line that a spark from a passing steam train once destroyed the roof, and the Meece Brook, where he drew fish and inspiration, runs for three miles alongside the track. The romantic age of the railway is manifest in spades as we pass through Crewe. The Italianate station buildings of this great junction are delightfully dark and decrepit, evoking a Dickensian age of steam. And part of the old railway works, where the blackberry-liveried giants of the Premier Line were built, were revived by the music entrepreneur Pete Waterman. In between appearances on *Pop Idol*, the former British Railways fireman recreated a boyhood dream, although the works he established are now owned by the train operating company Arriva.

Observant passengers may spot north of the station a futuristic but forlorn-looking train parked in the sidings. The paint is peeling, moss is growing round the window frames and its wheels seem rusted to the track. Once this was the most sophisticated train on the planet, a marvel of cutting-edge British technology to inspire the world. British boffins had invented a tilting train that could go round curves at high speed. At least that was the idea. Instead, the Advanced Passenger Train, as it was hubristically known, turned out to be a monument to British failure even greater than Eddie the Eagle. At the press launch in 1981 the invited hacks and dignitaries staggered off reporting horrible motion sickness. Whether this was the fault of the train itself or the effects of a large liquid lunch will never be known. But the British lost faith, let the Italians take over the technology and then spent a lot of money buying it back from them.

Now the light is fading, though as we pull out of Preston there might just be a chance to get a glimpse of the floodlit ethereal spire of St Walburge's church designed by Joseph Hansom, of Hansom cab fame, the third highest in Britain, after Norwich and Salisbury cathedrals. It is of just as much interest to railway enthusiasts as architectural historians, since the spire is made from sleepers recovered from the Lancaster and Carlisle Railway. Talk of sleepers inspires thoughts of bed, and it is getting late now. There are few greater pleasures than being rocked to sleep by the gentle motion of a train and slumber should be guaranteed. Unlike the first sleeping cars, introduced by the North British Railway in 1873, passengers are not required to bring their own bed linen. Though they should prepare for the jolt at Edinburgh in the middle of the night as a Class 67 diesel is marshalled onto the front of the train for the rest of the journey to Fort William.

At 5.50 next morning the sun is already up and Abdul is knocking on my door with my breakfast tray in his hand to whet an appetite for the start of what was voted in 2009 'the world's most scenic railway journey'. We are trundling through Westerton in the northern suburbs of Glasgow and the Clyde, to the left, is a far cry from the busy waterway depicted in the 1936 film *Night Mail*, where the grainy smoky river was packed with shipping as far as the eye could see. There are no 'steam tugs yelping down the glade of cranes' nor 'furnaces set on dark plains' as W H Auden put it in his famous film script. In fact, the riverbank is so bucolic this June morning that one could almost imagine you could cast a spinner for a trout without a single boat's wash getting in the way. But maybe it is a little early to get carried away by such innocent thoughts, since security fencing and barbed wire is coming into view along Gare Loch, a sign that we are approaching the huge Faslane naval base, home of the Trident submarine and Britain's nuclear deterrent.

Garelochhead station, at the beginning of Loch Long, is the start of the West Highland adventure proper, with its Swiss-chalet-style architecture and island platform the hallmarks of the line (so precise were the original engineers that some of the building materials were imported directly from Switzerland). One moment we are in the Lowlands and the next in the Highlands, as the train climbs steeply along the side of the loch. It's easy to imagine how the passengers marvelled in the brand new claret-coloured carriages on the first official train from Glasgow on Saturday 11 August 1894. As John Thomas puts it in his book *The West Highland Railway*, 'The visitors were gathering to celebrate an event unique in British railway history. That day there was to be opened ceremonially a main line through one hundred miles of mountain and moorland, with not a branch line nor scarcely a village worthy of the name in all its length.' 'It throws open to the public,' said the *Railway Gazette* at the time, 'wide and interesting tracts of country which have been almost as much unknown to the ordinary tourist as Central Africa was ten years ago.'

Even in the twenty-first century, awakening in a sleeper bed fresh up from London somehow makes the scenery seem oddly exotic as we head along Loch Long, past Loch Lomond, squeezing through Glen Falloch, past Crianlarich, junction for the Oban line, with its famous refreshment rooms, once so celebrated for their luncheon baskets that twenty miles on either side of the line used to be littered with champagne corks and the discarded shells of plovers' eggs. Then on through Strathfillan to Tyndrum and the lonely little station of Bridge of Orchy. Now we're on the long climb to the bleak 400 square miles of the Moor of Rannoch, the bleakest place in the British Isles. Here are stags in profusion, with towering antlers, staring curiously at the train on the treeless moors. The lifespan of most of them is destined to be short, since on 1 August the shooting season will open. Whatever your view on such a sensitive subject, it was the stags and the influence of the powerful owners of the estates along the lineside that probably saved the train when it was threatened with withdrawal shortly after privatisation, and provided the Deerstalker Express with its nickname. On to the highest point of the line at Corrour, 1,350 feet above sea level, then a swift descent down Loch Treigside and through the gorges of the Spean to Fort William at sea level on the banks of Loch Linnhe, in the shadow of Ben Nevis. As John Thomas writes, 'Never before in Britain had such a spectacular length of line been opened in one day. Never before had opening day guests been taken on so spectacular and exciting a trip. Here was a railway fascinating beyond words, every foot of it with a place in the past, a story in every mile.'

It is for the sake of one of these stories that I am not – unlike almost all my fellow passengers – continuing to the terminus at Fort William this morning. Instead, I am alighting at Rannoch, officially the loneliest station in Britain. Crunching on the gravel of the platform with my suitcase, I feel like Spencer Tracey in *Bad Day at Black Rock*, the only passenger to alight and seemingly the only living being on an uninhabited planet apart from a few hungry-looking peewits pecking at puddles in the gravel. For a moment there's a tightness at the back of the throat as I see nothing but a vast expanse of treeless boggy moorland and read a notice outside the station that proclaims, 'At 1,000 feet, Rannoch Moor provides one of the wildest and most forbidding landscapes in Britain – treacherous mires, boulder-strewn moorland, complete lack of shelter and exposure to wind and rain make this an inhospitable environment. Walkers are warned this is not an area to trifle with.'

It is beginning to rain, and suddenly I notice there's no signal on my phone. And there is no sign of the hotel I booked, a building once used to shield the construction workers on the line from the elements. Did I really book this place, or was I imagining it? When I do find the Moor of Rannoch Hotel there is an ominous notice on the door: 'Liz has broken her ankle and we are closed to non-residents.' But there is an enormous welcome from Liz Conway and her husband Rob, both Scousers who fell in love with the place on a holiday, restored it, gave up their jobs and are now in their seventh season running the hotel. 'Look on the map,' Liz tells me. 'It's as remote as can be. The nearest shops and garage are forty miles away. But the railway makes it not remote at all. And we never feel lonely. The train is everything to us. Do you know we get people, come up from Euston on the sleeper on Friday night and go back on the Sunday? It's a special little bit of solitude. But if the railway was ever threatened again, I don't know what we'd do.'

On a bleak winter's day back in 1889 a party of mostly middle-aged directors and contractors for the line got more solitude than they bargained for when they set out to cross the moor outside the hotel to scout out a possible route. They had clearly not read their Robert Louis Stevenson, who wrote in *Kidnapped* of Rannoch,

The mist rose and died away and showed us that country lying as waste as the sea; only the moorfowl and peewits crying over it and far to the east a herd of deer moving like dots. Much of it was red with heather; much of the rest broken up with bogs and hags and peaty pools; some had been burned black in a heath fire and in another place there was quite a forest of dead firs, standing like skeletons. A wearier-looking desert man never saw.

The sight of this preposterous group of Victorians stumbling around on the moor in their tweeds and umbrellas would have been comic if it hadn't nearly ended in tragedy after the men got lost in the sleet and darkness. They floundered, utterly disoriented in the desolate stormswept waste until rescued by shepherds many hours later.

By the time Liz Conway had cooked me a (second) vast breakfast, the moor looked sweet and friendly in the summer sunshine. I have come armed with Dr George Hendry's *Book of Midges*, whose wisdom is as essential as any guidebook in this part of the insect-filled Highlands, and head out onto the moor along the banks of Loch Laggan. Curiously it does not feel spongy at all, although there are many patches of water looking like black treacle spilled on the grass. Everywhere there are roots of old Caledonian Scots pine, like ancient bones pickled in the peat, from the forest that once stood here. But danger is never far away. Thomas Telford gave up the idea of building a road here when it appeared the bog would swallow up every piece of foundation you put in it. It nearly defeated the rail builders too. Every last bit of spoil from constructing the line tunnels was poured into the moor and still the bog gulped down everything until the builders had the idea of floating a layer of brushwood – much as Robert Stephenson had done with Chat Moss on the Liverpool and Manchester Railway. Even today some passengers swear they notice an extra bounce in the track as it passes across the moor.

Remote though it is, the main part of the West Highland line was not threatened by Beeching. There have never been more than five passenger trains on a normal day, but its future was safeguarded by an aluminium plant at Lochaber near Fort William, fed by cheap hydroelectricity and generating a steady freight flow, rare for a line built primarily for passengers. Not so for the beautiful extension running for forty-two miles from Fort William to Mallaig, which Beeching settled on with his beady eye until it was ultimately saved in 1995, helped by the unlikely enterprise of a north of England farmer called David Smith. Each year during the summer months Smith and his West Coast Railway Company run an invariably packed steam train daily up the line and back. It would have been especially ironic if the line had shut, since when it was built in the 1890s it was the first in Britain to get a public subsidy, now the lifeblood of almost every secondary railway in Britain. At the time MPs were concerned about the plight of the crofters and fishermen in the remote west of Scotland, which with reports of starvation and worse was the Third World of its day. Money was voted to build a line to get fish down from the coast to the markets in Glasgow and thus to stave off disaster. But where exactly should the line run? Someone stuck their finger on a map, found a speck with a bit of a harbour and so the railway builders created the nation's biggest herring port at Mallaig.

Arriving on the early train from Rannoch into the relative civilisation of Fort William after a day walking on Rannoch Moor seems a bit like how it must have felt for an immigrant from the west of Ireland to contemplate Manhattan for the first time. No time to pause in the fleshpots (even if there were any in this dour West Highland capital) because the 10.20 Jacobite train to Mallaig is already in the platform, with K1 Class locomotive No. 62005 *Lord of the Isles* already blowing off steam, its polished black livery making it look like a blackberry. The lithe K1 2-6-0s owe their pedigree to a design specially drawn up for the West Highland Line by Sir Nigel Gresley, and *Lord of the Isles* only escaped the scrapyard by hiding away as a stationary boiler in an ICI works in north-east England after being withdrawn from service by British Railways.

I'm travelling up to Mallaig with the loco's custodians, Gary, Ian, 'Malcy' and Neil, members of the North Eastern Locomotive Preservation Group, who love this piece of machinery so passionately that they have used up their annual holiday to ensure that no one neglects her maintenance. 'She's like a woman,' Malcy explains. 'She's beautiful, but she's quite capable of being temperamental and moody.' Each man will take a turn in the punishing work of firing over the predominantly 1 in 40 gradients, and they have their own reserved compartment in the train. On the door is a notice which reads: 'No admittance. Wear ear protection. Snoring in progress.'

There are fewer better descriptions of travel on the line than that of the humorist Miles Kington, who wrote in his book *Steaming through Britain*,

> What you have to bear in mind when setting off from Fort William to Mallaig is that you're going from sea level to sea level. The trip to Mallaig is like going across the back of a glove – you go a long way up and a long way down but every now and then you glimpse a long snake of water snaking down to the sea. It is this coexistence of wild mountain scenery and the invisible nearness of the sea which gives the Mallaig line its special flavour, which you don't get on the line up from Glasgow or even the Settle and Carlisle.

Driver Alec McDonald, who has been at the regulator since steam days on British Railways (you don't have to retire from driving steam trains as long as you are fit, and the oldest steam drivers are invariably the best, it is said), eases the loaded train past Ben Nevis and over the swing bridge across Thomas Telford's great Caledonian Canal at Banavie. Here is the radio control centre which directs all the trains from Mallaig to Glasgow. Once drivers had to swap a large leather token a bit like a horse's halter with the signalman every few miles. On the West Highland lines these tokens are now metaphorical, delivered over a radio telephone to the driver, and we stop at Glenfinnan for a virtual interchange with a train going south. Here at the head of Loch Shiel is a poignant memorial to Bonnie Prince Charlie, recalling the 1745 rebellion, which ended in tragedy at Culloden. There is a little museum on the station with a few artefacts from the old days on the line, and John Barnes, the shrine's curator, a serious, bearded Englishman, who has been one of the line's best friends over the past two decades, tells me that the figure on the top is not the Bonnie Prince himself, as many think, but an anonymous Highland chieftain sculpted by a friend of Walter Scott. Running across the valley is the mighty Glenfinnan Viaduct, 416 yards long with 21 curving arches set 100 feet above the ground – one of the world's most stunning engineering achievements and built entirely of concrete, though few would guess, so well does it blend in with its setting. Its builder Sir Robert McAlpine earned the nickname 'Concrete Bob' and until recently a diesel loco-motive named after him ran on the line.

But it's not the achievements of Concrete Bob nor the heritage of the Mallaig extension that attract people to travel on the Jacobite these days. I notice that many passengers, especially Japanese tourists, are pausing to press their noses against the window of our compartment. Malcy and Co. are smirking. 'Do you realise,' Malcy tells me, 'that you are sitting in Harry Potter's seat when they filmed the Hogwarts Express going over the viaduct?' As we pass over the vast structure, which has featured in three Harry Potter films, Neil says, 'Look on the opposite hillside over there.' And sure enough there's a phalanx of photographers with popping flashes, busy turning the viaduct into as much an icon of popular culture as Abbey Road. 'And there's probably barely a railway enthusiast among them!' says Gary. Eat your heart out, Bonny Prince Charlie!

Meanwhile Driver McDonald is making smart work of the 1

in 40 gradients, the bark from the exhaust ricocheting against the rocky sides of the cuttings – past Arisaig, Britain's most westerly station, and Morar with its white sands and grandstanding view across to the islands of Rhum, Muck and Eigg. Here is Scotland's deepest loch – 1,017 feet to the bottom – though maybe not the loneliest since like Loch Ness it is reputed to have its own monster.

In no time we're at the buffers in Mallaig. In the days when the town was one of the busiest herring ports in Europe you could hardly move for fish. Miles Kington writes,

> It fell out of every boat, every nook and cranny. If you wanted to cook a fish on your shovel on the way home, you just picked one up off the quay. There's the legendary story of the man at the station who asked the driver if there were any spare fish on board. Aye, third car down, he said. The man opened the door to the third car down and ten ton of fish fell on top of him.

Now there's hardly a herring to be seen, and if you are offered Mallaig kippers, they have probably been imported from Canada. These days it is the prawn fleet that rakes in the cash, though you will get the finest, flakiest and freshest haddock and chips any-where in the British Isles by going where the locals go – to the back doors of the cafes by the harbourside. I eat mine out of a brown paper bag on the quay, watching two fat seals creep up to a fishing boat, intent on larceny. I don't tell on them, partly because the hooter of 62005 is already blowing and passengers are scurrying back to the station for the train back to Fort William. I'm travelling back with Florence McLean, the 'Queen of the Jacobite', who is the guard, the master of ceremonies, the issuer of tickets and the mother figure for the 300 passengers who travel on the train every day between May and October.

'People in Fort William say, how did you get such a great job? It's the best job in the world. It's in my blood,' she tells me in the sweet local accent that is fast disappearing from the West Highlands these days. 'I was born and bred in the place, but I never tire of it – it's so green and so lush.' Florence has always been a pioneer. Back in the 1980s she was a freight guard on the line, quite an achievement in the macho west Scottish culture of the time. Nowadays, she tells me, life on the trains is just as tough, but there are many highlights: 'I love it when people get engaged on the train. I usually don't know in advance, but I announce it over the loudspeaker and deliver the champagne. I can't even relax on my day off because I worry about the train so much.'

But there is nothing to fret about tonight as *Lord of the Isles* eases the train gently into Fort William, the evening sun reflecting gold off Ben Nevis. In the next platform, freshly spruced up for tonight's journey home to Euston, is the Fort William portion of the Deerstalker Express. Once upon a time, before Beeching and the modern corporate railway, in backwaters and branch lines up and down the land, there were what might be termed the 'trains that Time Forgot': a couple of elderly main line carriages pensioned off from crack services, in the charge of a former express locomotive whose reason for existence had disappeared in the mists of time. The four coaches of tonight's train are a bit like this – two sleeping cars from the 1970s and a coach with seats of even earlier vintage which potters only as far as Edinburgh. But, hurrah, the fourth carriage is a restaurant car. It may be kitted out in the dated style of a mobile Angus Steak House, but where else on the entire railway would a full meal service be provided on such a diminutive train?

By the end of 2009, even on the crack expresses, proper dining on trains was all but extinct. The best you could hope for, even travelling from Penzance to Aberdeen, might be a cheeseburger or a microwaved curry. But tonight, on a train which probably carries at most forty passengers on a good day, here is Scotland's finest. Shhh, don't spill the secret. Fancy some haggis, neeps and tatties? Or Cumbrian lamb hotpot? Alison, who runs the place, has already put fresh flowers on the tables and started pouring from the widest selection of malt whiskies to be found on any train anywhere. 'If you want another wee dram,' she tells me, 'I'll be serving till we get to Edinburgh, past midnight.' And so I settle back with a Bruichladdich for one of the best views in the world, rolling gently through the Highlands, following the setting sun. And so we climb through the valley of the River Spean, black water shooting into white rapids, alongside the hauntingly lonely Loch Treig, with a final glimpse of Ben Nevis over our shoulders, climbing up to the bogland of Corrour, once a private station for the grand estate nearby, though now owned more democratically by two Harvard academics. It's starting to get dark now, I catch sight of the welcoming lights of the Moor of Rannoch Hotel before the train runs downhill all the way, past the crossing at Gorton, where once the local children went to school in a railway carriage because there was no road out, and round the famous Horseshoe Curve, where the train double backs on itself to squeeze round the twin peaks of Beinn Dorain and Beinn Odhar – a cost-saving exercise by the engineers which served to create one of Britain's most thrilling bits of railway.

As the last remnants of dusk float gently down over the West Highlands on this June night, the Deerstalker Express halts at Crianlarich, crossing a freight train of alumina tanks heading north. My sleeper is a carriage like those of old, with that rare luxury a pull-down window. I lean out for a final swig of the sweet Highland air before bed – a draught of champagne before the fug of the Euston Road in the morning. There is just a single passenger waiting on the platform – a portly red-faced Englishman, who for all I know has a brace of grouse in the trunk he is carrying. There's no other sound on the evening breeze except the soft Scottish chatter of the driver and his mate, who have stepped onto the platform awaiting their signal. It's reckoned that it costs £2 million a year in public subsidy to keep this train running. It is money well spent.

Little train, big journey: A single-carriage Class 153 unit
meanders through Knucklas on its way from Shrewsbury to Swansea
in May 2009. The service may be sparse, but it is one of the
great railway journeys of the world.

CHAPTER NINE

THE 14.05 FROM SHREWSBURY – SLOW TRAIN INTO THE 'UNPRONOUNCEABLE' HEART OF WALES

Shrewsbury to Swansea, via Craven Arms, Llandrindod Wells, Llangammarch Wells, Llanwrtyd Wells and Llanelli

A single railcar meanders through some of the richest and remotest countryside in Britain on its slow journey through the old counties of Shropshire, Radnorshire and Brecknock. No one is in much of a hurry here on the Heart of Wales Line. Somehow it seems to be permanently Sunday afternoon on this, the closest we have to the traditional rural railway of the Edwardian era. True, the thirty-four tiny stations with names that defy pronunciation by the English are now unstaffed and the sidings that once echoed to the clatter of milk churns and the cacophony of sheep on their way to market have long been lifted. But you are just as likely to run into Mrs Jenkins on the way to Llandrindod Wells to change her library books, or neighbour Dai alighting at Llanwrtyd for some of the local butcher's finest Welsh lamb chops and a couple of pints in the Neuadd Arms while waiting for the train home.

With only four services a day on the line, these are trains you don't want to miss – literally. My heart sinks like the axles on my main line connection from Birmingham as we run into flood-water outside Telford. Will I make it? I ring through to the station manager's office at Shrewsbury, hoping I can still catch the connection, but prepare for a long wet wait. As we limp in twenty minutes behind schedule, the little Heart of Wales train is still there, engines grinding in the bay platform. 'Hop along,' says John, the conductor-guard. 'We knew there were passengers on their way so we waited for you.' He adds, 'Don't worry, we've got hours to make up the time!' How refreshing to find an antidote to the anonymous world of the privatised railway, especially as the train I'm boarding is run under franchise by Arriva, one of the world's mightiest transport conglomerates, which carries two billion passengers a year in Europe alone.

In its day, the Heart of Wales too was an audaciously commercial enterprise. Built in 1868 as a long tentacle from Crewe to give the mighty London and North Western Railway access to industrial South Wales, it was a cheeky infiltrator onto turf which the Great Western believed to be its own. For much of its life it was dominated by heavy coal and mineral trains, but now you are more likely to spot the rare red kite that sometimes swoops overhead and rabbits scurrying over the tracks than a freight wagon. Once upon a time, laden passenger trains carried hundreds of thousands of city dwellers to take the waters at Builth Wells or Llandrindod Wells, genteel spa towns that owe their entire existence to the railway. It is hard to imagine now, as the line quietly settles back into its slumbers. It was slated for closure in 1963 but saved after a vigorous local campaign. It's said now that the line is unshuttable since it runs through six marginal constituencies, and it has a healthy and assured future, supported by the pro-rail policies of the Welsh Assembly and a vocal passenger group, the Heart of Wales Line Travellers' Association.

I'm well stocked up with food and drink, as this is one of the longest journeys in the land without refreshments being provided on the train nor available at stations on the way, although in the summer it is sometimes possible to get a snack as trains wait to pass at Llandrindod Wells. My little Class 153 railcar is generally clean, but like all British Rail-built coaches from the 1980s has high windows that are sometimes hard to see from, and the noise and vibration from the underfloor engines can be wearing. Despite the rain, this is high summer, and the trackside is lined with vegetation, reducing visibility over long stretches.

Luckily John the Guard is in chatty mood. Do passengers know that the towering signal box outside Shrewsbury is the biggest still operated manually by levers in the UK? And so it goes on as we head out on the main line to Newport, along gentle border valleys dominated by Wenlock Edge and the Shropshire Hills. John, it turns out, used to be a train builder at the famous railway works in Crewe. But Britain no longer makes many trains these days, so John, at sixty, has embarked on a new career, selling tickets, chatting up tourists and helping old ladies onto the platform. 'I spent twenty-nine years building trains like this. Then I was made redundant. But now after all this time I've found my true vocation. I'm a people person,' he says. 'But I still can't pronounce half the names of the stations down the line,' he says in a broad Cheshire accent.

At Craven Arms, the junction with the main line, the driver leans out to pick up the token that gives access to the seventy-nine miles of single track that will ultimately join the South Wales main line near Llanelli. There is water everywhere, with the fields flooded to Noah-like depths as far as the eye can see. A flag flutters on the medieval tower of Stokesay Castle, the finest fortified medieval manor house in England, and looks quite surreal above the waters. Here is the serene countryside of Housman's *A Shropshire Lad*, but it's also famous for its rabbits. I can't see any of them this morning. 'But you should be on the first train of the day,' says John. 'Hundreds of them, scurrying all over the track.' Soon we are in the handsome border town of Knighton, where the station is in England but the town centre in Wales. The hotel next to the station, it is said, was deliberately sited in England so that boozers could top up on Sundays in the days when Wales was dry on the sabbath. The driver gets out of his cab and pops into a little grey fibreglass hut on the platform. Not for a quick pee, as some passengers think, but because it's the housing for the magnificent old cast iron Tyer's token machine that controls the signalling on the line. The driver takes a large old key from the machine, obtaining permission to enter the next section to Llandrindod Wells. He can only do this after he's rung the signalman in the old Great Western Railway wooden signal box at Pantyffynnon, seventy miles to the south, which controls the whole line. No fancy radio signalling or computer technology here. This is good old primitive technology, fuelled by Welsh natter between drivers and signalmen, which prevents trains colliding head on in single-track sections. Old-fashioned and reliable, it still works as well as when it was invented more than a century ago.

Next stop is Knucklas, dominated by its grand viaduct, one of the most famous in Britain, taking the line on thirteen stone arches seventy-five feet above the Heyope valley. The castellated turrets reflect the style of the ruined castle on the hill nearby, although they are a bit of a sham – just hollow floor-less constructions and too unrealistic for any railwaymen with Walter Mitty-like tendencies to pretend they were taking part in a medieval siege. It's possible to see the viaduct from the train on the approach curve, although far better to get off and tramp up through the mud on the neighbouring hill. The local farmers are used to it. It's worth waiting between trains to take advantage of one of the best vantage points for photographing a country railway in the whole of Britain. Refreshment can be taken in the village's Castle Inn, whose landlord, a claret-faced former RAF officer, once opened up the pub early for me, just to have a chat. He told me that he had met his wife in a bar. 'She's a fantastic cook' – a view amply justified by the quality of a specially prepared lunch.

The line curves and climbs through the hills, past the remote halts of Llangynllo and Llanbister Road – the suffix 'Road' being one of the rural railway builders' great white lies, meaning 'It would have been too expensive to build the line to this obscure village, but intending passengers won't know they need hiking boots until they get there.' In the case of Llanbister Road, it's not even near the road to the village. Dolau's platform garden, lovingly planted out by local residents, is a blaze of glory. 'There are some great station gardens along here,' says John. 'But don't think I've got a cushy life just pottering up and down this line. I have to work on others too. I've already been to Chester and Aberystwyth in the past couple of days. And you try doing the last train out of Birmingham, with all the drunks on a Saturday night. And there are twelve request stops on this line – and sometimes I have to stop the train at nine of them.' Suddenly, there's a crunch and a grinding sound, and the emergency brake comes on. John leaps out onto the track and sprints up to talk to the driver. It turns out we have hit a small tree that has fallen across the line in the heavy rain. 'You think we staged this for your benefit,' he jokes. 'But there's no damage done. Tough trains these, you know. Remember I helped build them. Anyhow, you're in good hands with Tommo, the driver. He's a Crewe Alexandra fan, like me.'

At Llandrindod Wells the train changes guards and I say goodbye to John as he swaps platforms to head north on the next train and back home to Crewe. 'By the way, the toilet's blocked and there's no water. Just to let you know,' he says with a cheery wave. 'They'll get it sorted out at Swansea.' Llandrindod, the county town of Powys, is the only place of any size on the line and has an impressive railway station to match, although it's not all the real thing. The wrought-iron canopy comes from the demolished Pump House Hotel in the town and the passing loop in the platforms was only re-established after the Beeching cuts left the line bereft of proper places for trains to pass. In the 1960s Beeching also robbed the county of the Mid-Wales Line, which had a junction at Builth Road providing connections to the north and south. This rambling route, run by the old Cambrian Railway, may have seemed like a basket case to Beeching, who regarded most of Wales as a lost cause, doomed to decline. But how handy to have such a line now. The Welsh Assembly pays for a daily service from Cardiff to Holyhead, but it has to travel a circuitous route via the English borders. Llandrindod also sports a splendid restored signal box, which is a museum too. It's painted in the colours of the old Great Western Railway, causing much tut-tutting among railway enthusiast purists, who have long been suspicious of GWR imperialism. Although the Heart of Wales Line was part of the Western Region during British Railways days, it has always been proud Midland Region territory, say the fans, and should rightly be liveried in its maroon and cream colours. But at least there are toilets and a privately run booking office, the only one on the line. Llandrindod's Victorian villas and mansion blocks from the spa era look rather surreal in the middle of bare hills – a bit like a chunk of Chiswick or Hampstead plonked down in the middle of nowhere. The town has a slightly empty and run-down air these days, a far cry from the time when the railway would disgorge tens of thousands here to take the waters, parade fashionably round the streets and buy fancy provisions from the famous Central Wales Emporium. 'It's all the welfare people,' says the lady behind the counter in Pritchard's garage. 'First it was the hippies and now it's the welfare. They flock to the town. We've got all that unused hotel space, you see. You can still get a cup of the waters, you know. But not many do it these days. Might as well go down to Boots and get a bottle of Gaviscon.'

Pritchard's art deco garage, which resembles one of those idealised structures that small boys had in the golden age of motoring, has pumps on the pavement and a roll call of long-dead marques – Hillman, Humber and Sunbeam – in a sky-blue frieze along the roof. The garage is now run partly as a charity shop and partly as a shrine to its former owners. 'It still belongs to two of the former mechanics in the business who bought it years ago,' says the charity lady. 'Both the old boys are in wheelchairs now, and one has lost part of his foot. But they still run the local funeral business, and they fill up the hearse from the pumps on the pavement, which still work.' I wonder whether the secret of the brothers' long life is the spa waters, which can still be drunk from the spring in Rock Park and which, according to the *Llandrindod Wells Guidebook 1897*, can cure eczema, skin disease, bronchial ailments, gastritis, heartburn and diseases of the bladder and kidneys, including 'diseases of a tubercular nature'. But it warns, 'From two to six glasses should be taken before breakfast, and another in the forenoon. But not later in the day . . . Better stay at home than subject one's organisation to careless use of these waters.' And it's not much good going to the pub instead, since for a town of its size Llandrindod is notoriously short of them. In any case, with just three trains a day on the line dallying in the pub is not to be recommended and I must hurry back to the station to get the next train south.

Although the Heart of Wales ranks high in the league of the world's great rail journeys, some find it disappointing because the vegetation by the lineside often obscures the view. There may be a very good reason for this given the many hundreds of sheep in the fields by the lineside. But no matter that much of the journey is filtered through blurred hedging, there are so many little stations with their comings and goings that it is never possible to get bored. There's quite a bustle when we arrive at Builth Road, even though it is two miles from Builth Wells, the famous spa town and home of the Royal Welsh Show. But don't get off there expecting to take a quick swig of the waters or even get a sight of another famous curiosity of the town – one of the few post boxes in Britain with the insignia of King Edward VIII – unless you're prepared for a stiff hike.

Fortunately, the station here, which used to be called High Level, had a Low Level counterpart on the Mid-Wales Line, just downstairs. Even though Beeching did his best to wipe it from the map in 1962, the old station buildings survive as a pub called the Cambrian Arms, which is an excellent place to stop for passengers wanting a sup of something stronger than spa water. But stay on board because soon we will be rolling along the valley of the Irfon, where the waters sometimes appear to almost lap against the track, and into Cilmeri, where the monument to Lywelyn ap Gruffud, the last native Prince of Wales, killed in 1252, can be seen on the right. (Cilmeri was once known as Cilmery Halt, one of the last stations to carry the suffix before British Rail purged the word from the timetable in 1969.)

At Llangammarch, not only is the name slightly more pronounceable than some on the line, but for the thousands of visitors that were once brought here by train from all over Britain to take cures in the spa, the waters were said to be more drinkable. Once a busy freight siding here exported gallons of it by bottle, although by the time it was shunted and bashed through sundry marshalling yards to its final destination, it was said not to have tasted particularly nice. As we approach Llanwrtyd Wells we are in the heart of primrose country, rich in wildlife. I count a whole menagerie of peregrine falcons, curlews, ravens and buzzards in the sky overhead. It's a reminder that the Heart of Wales Line is best enjoyed slow, and I have chosen to take a break in the town overnight, for no other reason than it looks on the map to be roughly halfway down the line, and who could resist somewhere with an unpronounceable name in the middle of nowhere, claiming to be 'the smallest town in Britain'?

So small in fact that there appears to be nothing there, although I quickly realise that, like Llanbister and Builth, the town proper is a hike along the road. Here is a bank, a church and an old-fashioned chemist out of Happy Families, where I buy a toothbrush made of bristle that appears to have been in stock since the 1950s. The grocery has so little on the shelves it looks like something out of Iron Curtain Europe, and the bookshop has no staff, just an honesty box. The Neuadd Arms, where I am to stay, is a battered old boozer overlooking the main square, and by the door is a replica leopardskin hat and a plaque commemorating Screaming Lord Sutch, founder of the Official Monster Raving Loony Party, who was a fixture at dozens of by-elections, once scoring so many votes against Margaret Thatcher in her Finchley constituency that the national candidate deposit was raised to deter him. Sutch played his last gig at the Neuadd Arms before his suicide in 1999. The plaque reads, 'David Sutch (Screaming Lord) 1940–1999'.

Inside the dark bar over a pint of home-brewed Heart of Wales bitter, Dai the Barman says, 'He was a great guy. He used to be the official starter for the Man v. Horse Race. Look, we've got his autograph on the wall up there. Came up every year for it, he did. Can you imagine – a bloke has to race a horse over twenty-two miles? And do you know, the year after Sutch died a man won it. Amazing really. Mind you, he was a marine and a marathon runner.' Dai used to teach at the local school, but he tells me he's happy pulling pints these days. The pub brews 1,728 pints of ale a week in an outhouse round the back, he tells me. 'We're quite famous for our sports here, you know. We started the World Bog Snorkelling Championships right here in this bar.' He gives me an elaborate run-down of the rules, which involve completing two consecutive lengths of a sixty-yard water-filled trench cut out of a peat bog. Competitors must wear snorkel and flippers and complete the course using only conventional swimming strokes relying on flipper power alone. The race takes place every August Bank Holiday in the Waen Rhydd bog down the road from the pub. 'We have a lady champion now,' someone pipes up from the back of the bar. 'From Heckmondwike she is. Lots of good bogs in Yorkshire, I reckon.'

On the menu tonight, predictably, is lamb shank and chips, and there's a notice on the wall of the lounge bar declaring the local climate to be similar to Majorca or Tenerife. Hard to believe on this windy evening, but the atmosphere in the saloon is warm enough. I ask around about how to get to the famous Cynghordy Viaduct on the other side of Sugar Loaf Mountain. The 283-yard viaduct carries the line on eighteen arches over the valley of the Afon Bran. It ranks high in the pantheon of British railway wonders – up there with Ribblehead and Glenfinnan but less accessible than either. So remote is it that a brickworks was estab-lished near the site, and for decades its products were regarded as the finest engineering bricks in Britain. Like many of the great civil engineering features of the Heart of Wales Line it is difficult to appreciate from the train and is especially spectacular when seen from the hillside as the sun rises. 'I'll take you there myself in the morning, boy,' a voice pipes up from the other side of the bar. 'So long as you buy one of my raffle tickets.' It is an elderly gap-toothed farmer who turns up at six o' clock the next morning to take me there. Pure, undiluted Welsh generosity.

Back at Llanwrtyd Wells station later that morning, after a jolt-ing ride in an ancient Land Rover over hilly tracks only to find the viaduct swathed in mist, there is a problem. Dozens of passengers are pacing the platform. There are only two passing places on the entire railway, and the southbound train is stuck somewhere up the line because of the weather. The northbound service is sitting with diesels thrumming impatiently and people are grumbling about the wait. 'Why so many on the train?' I ask the conductor. 'Oh, it's like this every day, you know. The Welsh Assembly give all the over-sixties free travel on the trains wherever they like, and sometimes it's like a Darby and Joan outing here.' Curiously it turns out that the conductor is called Joan herself, and confesses she is sixty-two. ' I used to run my own mail order business with my husband, but the stress got to me and I decided to downshift. The old man's now a postman, and he's much happier too.' Unlike some of the stations on the line, which are shuttered and desolate, Llanwrtyd, although unstaffed, is a pretty place, with immaculate gardens and plenty of evidence of the railway as it once was. The wooden board from the old LMS signal box has been repainted and has prime position above the flower bed. In the days of steam, engines used to take water here, and you can still see the grating for the surplus water at the end of the platform. Steam locomotives still occasionally pass this way on special trains, but now they are filled up by the local fire brigade.

After nearly an hour we are off. The driver picks up the token for Llandovery and sets off for the three-mile climb on a 1 in 60 gradient for Sugar Loaf summit at 820 feet. The single-car diesel makes light work of it, but in steam days, with an LMS Class 8F freight locomotive in charge of a long train of coal wagons, it was a stiff test of a fireman's endurance, particularly as it was followed straight away by the plunge into the 1,001-yard Sugar Loaf Tunnel, a dark melancholy place plagued by swirling steam and roof falls. The tunnel marks the boundary, not just between the counties of Powys and Carmarthenshire, but also between two distinct weather zones. Although it was drizzling as we entered the tunnel, perversely, the sun is shining as we run gingerly onto the Cynghordy Viaduct. It is just possible to see Sugar Loaf itself on the left behind the train, and keen-eyed passengers will spot red kites wheeling overhead, making a change from the ubiquitous sheep – for this is forestry country. Through the little Cynghordy station ('Not many requests for this one,' Joan tells me) and the next twenty miles are downhill, although 'gently does it' because much of it is undertaken squealing round curves. Past Llandovery, a boozers' paradise for more than half a millennium, where drovers slaked their thirst in the town's many pubs thanks to a special licence granted by the lord of the manor (the tradition is still continued by the supporters of the local rugby club known as the Drovers). Then on to Llandeilo with its colour-washed houses in the lee of the big Victorian church on the hillside.

Soon we are in industrial South Wales, much of it post-industrial now, with the scars left by former metalworks and collieries and the cat's cradle of tracks that once served them now almost all a memory. And, hurrah, here is the signal box at Pantyffynon that controls the entire line right up to Craven Arms – not some bland Network Rail construction, but a grand old Great Western Railway timber and brick building from 1892. It still has its finials on the roof and the paint is peeling authentically. At Llanelli we meet the junction with the main line, where the train reverses. Once it would have gone on directly to Swansea Victoria, the original London and North Western terminus of the line, but this was closed by Beeching in 1964 and is now a leisure centre. Llanelli was once known as 'Tinopolis' and famous a century ago as the largest town in the world where more than half the population spoke a Celtic language. The train sprints along the main line to Swansea's old Great Western station, where the journey ends modestly at the buffer stops. On the way back I bump into John the Guard. 'I've been looking out for you along the line all day,' he tells me. 'We were stuck at a signal at the junction at Craven Arms for more than two hours as the floodwaters rose.' 'Were the punters panicked?' I ask. 'Not a chance,' he says. 'I kept them amused by getting them to count sheep!' It seems inconceivable now that this remotest of backwaters once dispatched its own daily express trains direct to London. But nowadays we must give thanks that the line still exists at all.

The train that ran on the road: 'Class 33' No. 33116 eases
its way along Weymouth Quay past a Hants and Dorset 'Bristol'
double-decker in August 1987 on a boat train connecting
with the Channel Islands ferry.

CHAPTER TEN

THE 08.41 TO CASTERBRIDGE, VIA *TESS OF THE D'URBERVILLES*

Bristol to Weymouth, via Trowbridge, Westbury, Yeovil Pen Mill, Maiden Newton and Dorchester

If there ever were a fantasy league of closed railway lines, the Somerset and Dorset would have to be at the top. Running from Bath over the rolling gradients of the Mendip Hills to Bournemouth on the Dorset coast, it has generated more melancholy, more nostalgia and a greater sense of loss than any other of the lines that Beeching closed, and probably all those that went before. Even prior to the Beeching era it was a kind of Holy Grail among railway lines. To have travelled on the Pines Express on a summer Saturday, loaded with holidaymakers from the factories and cotton mills of Lancashire and the Black Country over the gradients to Bournemouth behind one of the heavy S & D 2-8-0 locomotives designed especially for the route, was said to have been an almost mystical experience. Just before it closed John Betjeman did a television documentary about it. 'Poor Evercreech is out of reach,' he eulogised, 'now the Pines does not pass through.' An eccentric photographer named Ivo Peters spent years before the closure driving up and down the line in his vintage Bentley to try to recreate the atmosphere, and his work has added to the continuing mystique surrounding the railway. On the weekend of closure in 1966 thousands of people flocked to the line to travel on the final trains. These were pursued by streams of cars and almost every bridge and vantage point was packed to bursting. 'As dusk fell on the evening of Sunday 6 March,' wrote the line's historian Robin Atthill, 'two Southern Pacifics stormed their way up to Masbury summit with their nine-coach special. I watched the red tail lamp of the train disappear into the darkness. Only a minute before, I had seen a glowing pillar of fire racing through Binegar . . . This was the end . . . I had watched the line die.'

Even though the headquarters of the Somerset and Dorset were at Glastonbury, there is no alchemy, no superhuman power that can bring it back – the trackbed is severed, modern housing estates and new roads obstruct the route – and the trains will never run again. But wait. In the rush of nostalgia we have forgotten about the other Somerset and Dorset. The one that Beeching didn't close, which runs parallel just a few miles away and is equally charming, just as picturesque and just as much a period piece as its long-departed sister. And although Beeching managed to axe some of the intermediate stations, it still, incredibly, has eight services a day in both directions. This morning my journey will take me from Bristol to Weymouth, via Bath, Trowbridge, Frome, Bruton, Castle Cary, Yeovil Pen Mill, Yetminster, Chetnole, Maiden Newton and Dorchester – literally the heart of Wessex, the old kingdom of the West Saxons, revived by Thomas Hardy as his 'dream country'. The line runs for eighty-seven miles through serene river valleys, rolling pasturelands and traditional market towns, as quiet today as when it was opened in 1857.

From Bristol it runs first through the deep, green Avon Valley, winding between the river and the Kennet and Avon Canal, through the ancient weaving town of Bradford-on-Avon. The valleys are left behind for the wide flat Wiltshire plain, past the famous Westbury White Horse, carved on the chalk hillside, and into the cider country of Somerset. Near here is Cadbury Castle, reputed to be King Arthur's Camelot, and everywhere on the horizon are the spires of honey-coloured churches, built with the wealth from the wool trade. At Yeovil the train passes into Hardy country, with several of the little stations having a counterpart in the Wessex novels and poems. The most famous is Casterbridge (Dorchester) where the house on which Hardy based Mayor

Henchard's home in the novel is now Barclay's Bank, and the King's Arms, through whose window Mrs Henchard spied her husband again after he sold her, is still one of the busiest hotels in the town. We also pause at Maiden Newton, famous as the Chalk Newton of *Tess of the D'Urbervilles*. Passing the great hill fort of Maiden Castle, celebrated as the title of a famous novel by that other great Wessex novelist John Cowper-Powys, the railway sweeps over the Dorset Downs to the World Heritage Site of the Jurassic Coast, and two hours and fifteen minutes later arrives at Weymouth, George III's favourite spot for dipping his toes in the water. This timeless, meandering railway is a backwater to a back-water, and a conduit to some of the most hidden places in England. In many senses we must be grateful the old S & D passed away because it ensured the Bristol to Weymouth line would live on. In the modern world there never would have been room for both of them.

The first through train south of the day from Bristol Temple Meads doesn't run until as late as 08.41. But it is a very special service, because the normal two-car Class 150 diesel train has an air-conditioned Class 158 unit attached to it. It may not seem much, but this is a notch up in the hierarchy of the mostly elder-ly diesel multiple units that operate the secondary services in the West Country. The extra carriages have been laid on today to take the volunteers who help to keep the line running to a special meeting in Dorchester, where they will be entertained by the management of the train company. At each little station along the line this morning, the local volunteers will climb aboard. These are the people who pull the weeds and paint the seats and who wear out their shoe leather pushing timetables through the doors of local people who believe the line must surely have closed forty years ago.

Already on board at Bristol are the ranks of the hierarchy of First Great Western, who have detached themselves from their grand offices next to the statue of Brunel in Paddington to get the 'red-eye' train to Bristol. Here is Mark Hopwood, the managing director himself, and his regional manager Julian Crow, along with assembled functionaries from Head Office. It is a bit like the humblest branch line being honoured with the presence of the old Great Western's Sir Daniel Gooch and Isambard Kingdom Brunel themselves, or the archbishop of Canterbury coming to wash the feet of poor parishioners on Maundy Thursday. (Although some-one tells me, 'The general manager is a bit of a gricer himself.')

I'm to be met by Catherine Phillips, the rail partnership officer, who people say could fuel the engines of the trains with her enthusiasm for the line. 'I'm a large lady with a lot of leaflets,' she tells me. 'You can't mistake me.' And she is just as I imagine her, a bit like a cross between Joyce Grenfell and Clarissa Dickson Wright. Which she needs to be since her job is to chivvy support for the line and keep the passenger numbers up. 'Up 163 per cent in six years,' she boasts. 'I used to be in the perfume business but I lost my appetite for the corporate world.' But she can't hold back her admiration for the top brass who have come to rally the volunteers today. 'When they put in for the franchise, they can't have wanted a backwater like this. A little line like this must be less than 2 per cent of their income,' she says.

There is always a heart-stopping moment when the branch line train swings off the main line onto its own tracks. What mysteries lie ahead? What prospects might unfold as we head down the *tiddly-dee, tiddly-da* tracks into the countryside? For the first part of the journey we are in Bristol and Bath commuterland, although no less attractive for that, running alongside the River Avon and the Kennett and Avon Canal. The volunteers are already talking up the line's virtues. They are a curious crew. Here's Michael, a former British Airways pilot, neat in suit and goatee beard, who runs the team of forty volunteers, and his deputy David Greening, who is a stress engineer at the Agusta Westland helicopter plant in Yeovil. Here too is Terry Gough, a professor of forensics at King's College London, and Norman from the Ramblers' Association, who organises walks from remote stations. It is clear that all these men and women love the line with a passion that cannot easily be explained.

David Greening, proud of his award as the 'railway volunteer of the year', tells me he has been supporting the line since he was a boy, when he wrote to transport minister Barbara Castle, deploring the possibility of its closure. There's little he doesn't know about the history of the line, including how it was planned by an independent company, the Wiltshire, Somerset and Weymouth, back in 1845 with the backing of the Great Western. 'Sorry about the track. You'll find some of it is in a pretty terrible state, particularly as we get farther down the line,' he tells me as we lurch through Avoncliff. 'But look at the fabulous view.' He points out at the frothing waters of Claverton Weir and then explains the line was a battlefront in the turf war between the Great Western and its rivals at Waterloo, the London and South Western and its successors the Southern Railway.

> The Great Western wanted to push their broad gauge as far
> as possible into the West Country and eventually they put
> Brunel in charge of building the line. Hard to believe it
> now, but this was a main line once, and a very lucrative
> one. It gave the Great Western access to a south coast port
> for trade with the Channel Islands and France. Until the
> 1960s the line was full of great Channel Islands boat
> expresses and freight trains loaded with fruit and flowers.
> And it's still important now for strategic reasons.

He winks at me conspiratorially. 'You know, the old Portland naval base – you never know when they might want to bring it back into use and run supplies there. Why do you think they've put new signals in at Yeovil? Hmm?'

We're now bouncing through Freshford and it's standing room only – a jolly middle-class church fete atmosphere. Catherine points out the station garden, where nearly everyone in the village has contributed a planting. At Bradford-on Avon the platform seats still have the original cast-iron ends displaying the crest of the Great Western Railway in its pre-1923 incarnation, along with the original stone buildings, and unlike most of the stations on the line there is still someone to sell you a ticket. As well as its prettiness, this, like many other rural secondary lines, is a lifeline for the disenfranchised – schoolchildren, students, the elderly who cannot afford a car. And just like the Somerset and Dorset of old, it still carries heavy summer traffic. 'Not everyone goes on holiday by car or aeroplane, you know,' Catherine says. 'We still have huge numbers of people in the summer, and they have to lay on locomotives specially to haul the trains. Then it's standing room only.'

It's not quite like the 1950s and 1960s when twelve-coach trains had to have a second engine to push them up the gradients. Like many lines, it was never able fully to recover from the economies imposed by Beeching. Hard to believe, as we bump and rattle over the non-welded track through Trowbridge, Wiltshire's county town, that the line had its heyday as recently as 1960, when Waterloo withdrew from Channel Islands services and the Heart of Wessex line had the traffic to itself – full to capacity with expresses. This was the height of the trainspotting era, and boys on their summer holidays were out in force to 'cop' the elusive Counties, the last class of main line steam engines designed by the Great Western Railway, which worked many of the last expresses on the line. It looked finally as though the Great Western had won its battle with Waterloo. But then came calamity. Running through an area of thin population with no heavy industry, the Heart of Wessex was a prime target for the Beeching axe. The names of the stations that closed in 1966 are an evocative rollcall of rural Dorset – Evershot, Marston Magna, Grimstone and Frampton and Bradford Peverell. No longer would even the slowest trains stop there. Worst of all, Dorchester West, the station serving the county town, was to close, although it was later reprieved. Much of the line was cut back to single track, transforming it at a stroke from a main line to a back route. But at least it didn't suffer the fate of the old Somerset and Dorset. There are still conspiracy theorists who claim that Great Western dirty tricks were at work and that the Paddington bosses were rubbing their hands at the closure of their old rival.

'Nonsense,' says David Greening. 'Brunel designed this line and it was simply the better engineered.' And here is the evidence, as we roll to a halt at Frome, where the great man's station, with its wooden overall roof, stands perfectly preserved and newly repainted in the old Great Western colours of chocolate and beige. 'All our own work,' says David. The volunteers have played a big part in the restoration of the station, which not long ago was in danger of falling down. (All this volunteering is not surprising, really, since all these little Avonside towns are in the heart of middle-class Middle England.) 'The station's in museum condition, now,' says David. Maybe so, but even Brunel's genius was not unflawed. The Great Western had to back down in the gauge war when the company was forced to concede that 7-foot ¼-inch track was not what the rest of Britain wanted. The line was converted to Robert Stephenson's 'narrow' gauge in 1874, using the labour of 1,800 navvies. The railway company sustained them with straw for bedding, along with coal and copious quantities of oatmeal which the navvies brewed into their favourite non-alcoholic drink, barley water.

The quality of the job is borne out by the high speed trains racing past us on their way to Exeter and Penzance. When the Great Western wanted to speed up its services to the west at the end of the nineteenth century, constructing a shorter way to bypass Bristol, it chose to co-opt part of the route of the Heart of Wessex line. We continue to jostle with the expresses through Bruton, a stone's throw from the old Somerset and Dorset station at Cole, where neat children play in front of the ancient chapel at King's Bruton school, and on to the junction at Castle Cary, a sleepy wool town, where a red kite hovers lazily over the track. It is possible to change onto the fast train to Paddington here, although progress is slower on foot to the village, which is a mile away.

Glastonbury Tor, floating like an island, with its roofless tower perched on the top, can be seen to the right. Was this peculiar-looking hill really the home of the king of the fairies and the entrance to the underworld? Or the place to which the Holy Grail was borne? There is little time to speculate as we rattle off the main line to take the single track down in the direction of Weymouth. This is rich pastureland, with fat cattle basking in the fields all the way to Yeovil, the only town of any size on the line. Here is the perfect country junction in a time warp. Once there were three stations in this small town, famous for its glove making, and there are still two: Yeovil Junction, on the Waterloo to Exeter main line, which crosses here, and Yeovil Pen Mill, where we pull up at a perfect set of Great Western lower quadrant semaphore signals. Once a little train linked the two stations; now passengers wanting to change have to get the bus or walk, even though the connecting railway tracks still exist. Not an enticing prospect after dark. But we must not complain, since Pen Mill has an exquisite flavour of the past – a working signal box surrounded by boxes of flowers, along with old-fashioned levers for raising and lowering the signals. There are rows of neat sidings, wrought-iron and glass canopies on the platforms and a charming little overbridge.

Too good to simply pass through, and I get off to say goodbye to Catherine Phillips, who is to pick up her car here. 'What's so special about this line,' she says, 'is the sense of place, don't you think? It just feels right in the landscape.' But there is a minor drama. A young couple stand disconsolately in the ticket office, having just missed their train. 'Where do you want to go?' Catherine asks them. 'I'll drive you. There won't be another train along till heavens knows when.' Can any volunteer have more love for their local line than this? 'And by the way,' she says to me, waving farewell as she drives away with her charges, 'don't forget to see Jack.' Jack? 'Yes, he's the station cat. Just knock on the signal box door. That's where he lives.' And, sure enough, he is there sprawled on the steps – a broad-faced black and white tom, basking in the sunshine. I could swear he smiled at me.

There are few better evocations of the country railway than Yeovil, and even two hours pass quickly at an old-fashioned station on a sunny late summer's afternoon. But I must move on. I settle into a corner of the carriage on the next train south, taking me through some of the most charming villages on the line – Thornford, Yetminster and Chetnole. All are halts, where passengers have to flag down the driver to stop the train. Thornford and Chetnole are simply concrete platforms in the middle of fields, but at Yetminster, in the centre of the village the stationmaster's house has been splendidly restored as a private residence. The train pauses at Maiden Newton to let another pass in the loop, and the conductor announces, 'We're going to be a few minutes, so anyone who wants to get off to stretch their legs and have a fag can do so.' Apart from me, the only person to alight in the warm afternoon sunshine is a young woman in hiking shorts, who is studying a map and looks far too healthy to want a cigarette. I can't help thinking of Edward Thomas's famous poem 'Adlestrop' – listening to a bird singing its heart out in the elder bush on the down platform. 'And for that minute a blackbird sang / Close by, and round him, mistier / Farther and farther, all the birds . . .' What sort of bird this one is I am not qualified to tell, but I am also reminded of Hardy's poem 'The Darkling Thrush', for Maiden Newton is 'Hardy Central'.

Thomas Hardy had a long-standing connection with the railways, from the time when, as a young surveyor in the 1860s, he supervised the removal of thousands of bodies from the graveyard of St Pancras Old Church when the Midland Railway extended its line to London. Among them was the body of the archbishop of Narbonne, which reportedly had a full set of porcelain false teeth.

Hardy reportedly found the whole experience a gruesome one. Schoolchildren through the ages have recited Hardy's railway poems 'Faintheart on a Railway Train' and 'At the Railway Station, Upway', and with his young wife Emma he was reportedly fond of taking the train to travel round Somerset and Wiltshire. In 1886 he wrote to his friend the critic Edmund Gosse inviting him to Dorchester to travel to some of the places 'newly opened up by the railway'. It turned out to be an unfortunate experience. The two men were stuck on the platform here at Maiden Newton for so long after missing their connection on the Bridport branch that Gosse told later how he had had the time to write a lengthy essay on his friend's poetic mentor William Barnes.

This little village station is almost unchanged since Hardy's day, retaining nearly all its stone Brunel buildings, although it is much quieter since the nine-mile Bridport branch closed in 1975. The days of Hardy and Gosse are long gone, and it is no longer possible to pass the time of day watching the Bridport branch train idling in the bay platform: 'A pannier tank coupled to its "B" set standing under the overall roof in the branch bay with smoke drifting lazily from the chimney,' wrote the historian of the line, Derek Phillips.

A faint breath of steam swirling from the safety valves. The driver would be wandering around the engine complete with his oil feeder, giving the straps and glands a top-up, and there is the scrape of a shovel on the footplate, as the fireman puts a few rounds of coal around the firebox whilst waiting for the rumble and the roar of an approaching main line stopping train. Carriage doors would slam as passengers disembark and head for the branch train, the boards would be 'off' and with a roar from the chimney as the vacuum ejector was opened and with a toot on the whistle, the pannier tank would pull away on the journey to Bridport, leaving a lingering smell of hot oil and steam in its wake.

While I wait, I don't spend my time writing a memoir like Gosse, but instead I walk part of the way along the old trackbed of the Bridport line, now converted into a cycleway. Here, their growth now uninhibited by passing trains, are those old-style denizens of dry railway embankments – tangles of evening primroses with their pale yellow flowers, and colonies of the snapdragon-like toadflax, with their yellow hoods and orange bulges like Adam's apples. And there is a bit of industrial archaeology too – old lengths of Brunel's original broad-gauge track still used as fence supports by a local farmer.

At the next station, Dorchester West, a group of men with a large Tesco bag overflowing with cans of Foster's lager are the only people on the down platform. This station was once nominated by the *Daily Telegraph* as the worst in Britain. 'No use waiting here, mate,' they shout across at me as I get off and pause to look at the timetable. 'There won't be another train along for two hours.' This used to be rather a grand place, with an overall roof and vast sidings that would echo to the bleating of sheep, the baying of cattle and the hue and cry of one of the busiest market towns in the south-west. All was swept away in the 1960s, but the elegant Italianate station building is still there, once housing first- and second-class waiting rooms. Even the booking office was partitioned so first- and second-class passengers didn't have to rub shoulders. Now it is an Indian restaurant, and as I wait for the final train of the day I try the Wednesday night special (£8.95 for three courses). The Alishaan is bright and cheerful in contrast to the gloom on the unstaffed platforms. Over a chicken shashlik in what was once the ticket hall, I ask the owner Mr Ali whether he gets people in trying to book for a journey. 'Dozens every day,' he says. 'If I am in a good mood, I let them in to use the toilet. If I am in a bad mood, I kick them out.' Grass grows high between the tracks as I wait for the train on the final leg of my journey. But half-close your eyes and it is just possible to imagine the packed Channel Islands Boat Express steaming into the platform from Paddington.

Sadly, the most evocatively named station on the line, Upwey Wishing Well Halt, closed in 1957, and the final station, Weymouth, is nondescript and modern – not much of a gateway to this elegant Georgian resort. This is also the terminus of the old Southern Railway line from Waterloo and the destination for the very last regular main line passenger steam trains in Britain in 1967. The Great Western had long lost its steam trains, so after all the battles of the rival companies to Weymouth, Waterloo had the last hurrah. But the journey does not quite end there. Buried under a tangle of ragwort and buddleia, the rusted tracks of a branch line disappear around the back of the station beyond a set of level crossing gates. This was once the Weymouth Harbour Tramway, where until the 1990s express boat trains would edge their carriages past holidaymakers in the town's narrow streets and quays to deposit their passengers alongside the Channel Islands ferries. Opened by the Great Western in the 1860s, it was the only street railway in Britain ever to carry regular main line passenger trains and was originally constructed in broad gauge, although Brunel's wide trains must have caused consternation on the narrow quays of the town. Theoretically it could carry trains now, although the last actual train operated in 1999, when a special tour ran from London. I follow the tracks round the back of the B & Q car park, and apart from the cars parked on the tracks in defiance of modern notices telling them not to, the line is intact, its rails worn shiny, not from rail use but from the regular motor traffic that passes over it. On the quayside, the little pannier tanks that operated it had bells to warn pedestrians, and the engine crews were known to be specially strong-armed, lifting parked cars out of the way. The lines are still intact and weed-free right up to the ferry terminal, although it is a long time since daffodils and Jersey potatoes were loaded into wagons to be sped up to London. Weymouth is to host the sailing events at the 2012 Olympics and some hope the line might see trains again as a green way to get spectators to the harbour front. 'Should it happen?' I ask a group of fishermen parking their catch, including a giant conger eel, in the middle of the tracks on the Old Harbour. 'You've got to be joking,' says one of the men, who has what seems to be an even more monstrous conger tattooed on his back. 'It's bad enough along here already. The last thing we need is a load of trains getting in our way. Green? It's a load of b******. Look what they've done to the fishing industry in the name of being green!' Until the 1960s this little railway was bustling. Now it looks unlikely that wheels will ever turn here again. Catherine and David and Norman and Terry and the other Heart of Wessex volunteers might hope that one day loaded trains might race down the tracks from Paddington, unloading cargoes of passengers in exchange for fresh flowers, fruit and vegetables from the fertile fields of Jersey and Guernsey. Sadly, like the revival of the Somerset and Dorset, here is another dream that seems destined to die.

Where time stands still: A moment for a gossip on the
single platform at the remote station of Berney Arms in 1947.
With no road access, this tiny Norfolk community is still
reliant on the few trains that stop here.

CHAPTER ELEVEN

THE 08.04 FROM NORWICH – 'SECRET' LINES TO LIVERPOOL STREET, VIA BRITAIN'S SMALLEST MAIN LINE STATION

Norwich to London Liverpool Street, via Buckenham, Berney Arms, Lowestoft and the East Suffolk Line through Beccles, Saxmundham, Woodbridge and Ipswich

'On Wednesday last, a respectably dressed young man was seen to go into a London station and deliberately take a ticket to Cambridge. He has not been heard of since.' So wrote *Punch* in the early 1860s, lampooning the awful train services of the Eastern Counties Railway, the company that in mid-Victorian times ran most of the trains to East Anglia. The novelist William Makepiece Thackeray commented at the same time in a similar sardonic vein, 'Even a journey on the Eastern Counties Railway comes to an end.'

But perhaps we should be grateful for East Anglia's remoteness and relative inaccessibility. It still has dreamy branch lines and slow secondary railways of the sort that disappeared from much of the rest of the network long ago. True, some of the quieter branches have gone. It's no longer possible to change at country junctions onto little two-coach trains pulled by antiquated engines for stations with lovely East Anglian names such as Lavenham, Brightlingsea, Aldeburgh, Southwold or Snape. No longer do trains loaded with holidaying mill workers from the West Midlands halt at Melton Constable and all stations beyond on their way to the holiday camps and camp sites of the Norfolk and Suffolk coasts. But there still are slow trains to be discovered on byways with quaint titles like the Bittern Line, the Poppy Line and the Wherry Line – 'winding slow' as John Betjeman put it 'to some forgotten country town'. Astonishingly, the East Suffolk Line (which does not have a nickname but is as lovely as any of them) still has direct trains from Lowestoft to London, stopping at stations in slumbering market towns on quiet river estuaries, much of the way on a single track.

It is tempting to hope that the managers up at Liverpool Street may still be oblivious to the lines beyond Cambridge, and that trains will somehow continue to chug in obscurity through quiet fenland stations in a parallel universe for ever more. But the survival of East Anglia's remaining branch lines has been hard won and communities are ever vigilant. None more so than around the little triangle of lines from Norwich to Yarmouth and Lowestoft, where local people have fought to preserve trains to both the smallest station in Britain and the station which has just about the tiniest passenger numbers of any in the land.

This morning I'm travelling to both, through remote marshes dotted with windmills and pretty riverside villages, underneath the 'big skies' so characteristic of Norfolk. It could not be a more perfect autumn day for such a journey. The early-morning sun is warming the spire of Norwich cathedral and firing up the red-brick frontage of Norwich Thorpe station. With its huge French elliptical dome and cupola, complete with classical urns, the terminus looks more like a chateau than anything as prosaic as a railway station in the bright morning light. Screw up your eyes and we could be on the River Loire rather than the plain old River Wensum. The pedimented clock on the roof says precisely eight o'clock, and the two-coach diesel forming the 08.04 Wherry Line train to Yarmouth is ready to leave.

First stop heading east is Brundall, on the banks of the River Yare and famous for its boatbuilding as well as being the home of Colin Chapman, the founder of the Lotus sports car firm. But it is neither boats nor fast cars I have come to see today. I am on my way to the remote platforms at Buckenham, which has an ignoble place in the statistics books as one of the least-used stations in Britain. According to the latest figures from the Office of Rail Regulation (whether you believe them or not) only ninety-seven passengers use the station each year, a statistic which must be directly related to the number of services that stop there. According to the timetable, the next train doesn't stop at Buckenham for another five days. 'The trouble with travelling on slow trains to small stations,' observes Ian Dinmore, Norfolk County Council's community rail officer, when I ring him to enquire about the service, 'is that they tend to be infrequent and infrequently stop.' Quite so. It appears I have no alternative but to walk from the previous station along the line.

To help me on my way, I am fortified with a mug of very strong railwaymen's tea in the porters' room at Brundall, one of the very few rural stations in Norfolk still to have a staff. There's Barry the crossing keeper, Roger the signalman and Steve the ticket collector, plus two others who relieve them on shifts. With its ornate wooden signal box, semaphore signals, fancy finials, wooden level crossing gates and stationmaster's house still intact, it probably comes as close as we can get in modern times to the idyll of the country station in its heyday, as atmospherically described by David St John Thomas in his book *The Country Railway*.

Calves, day-old chicks, pigs and other reinforcements for the local livestock normally came in by passenger train along with the mails, newspapers and local soldiers on leave. The pair of rails disappearing over the horizon stood for progress, disaster, the major changes in life; the route to Covent Garden and Ypres, the way one's fiancé paid his first visit to one's parents, one's children returned for deathbed leavetaking . . . The country railway provided more than transport. It was always part of the district it served, with its own natural history, its own legends and folklore, a staff who were at the heart of village affairs, its stations and adjoining pubs places for gossip news and advice.

That world has not entirely vanished from the Wherry Line, which is still run almost entirely with equipment from the Victorian era. 'That's why it's so special,' says Barry, stroking an Ancient Mariner beard and speaking over the rattle of teaspoons stirring large quantities of sugar into mugs. A chiming clock periodically interrupts our conversation. 'We do it the old way – the semaphores, the manned crossings, the mechanical locking systems of the signals and points. We even have a man who comes round each week to fill up the paraffin in the signal lamps and on the crossing gates.' Barry reels off the list of signal boxes on the line, all of which still have a human being to pull levers attached to wires that change the points and raise and lower the signals – Yarmouth, Acle, Brundall, Cantley, Reedham, Somerleyton – a recitation which goes on until Roger pings the bell from the signal box, and it is time to swing closed the heavy wooden level crossing gates to let a train pass. 'The old ways are the safest,' muses Steve. Although he's not entirely right, since on a rainy night on 10 September 1874 a tragic accident happened near here, when the mail train from Yarmouth crashed at speed into an express from London, killing twenty-five and injuring more than a hundred others. 'One of the most appalling accidents that ever happened in English railway history,' reported the *Illustrated London News* at the time, and it remains so to this day. The graves of the driver and fireman of the mail train can still be seen in the Rosary Cemetery, Norwich.

Buckenham station is so little used that the Ordnance Survey have not even bothered to put it on my map, but it does not seem to matter on this mesmerising walk from Brundall along deserted country lanes lined with holm oaks and sloe bushes. Shiny blueberries and fat bullaces – a speciality in this part of Norfolk – are everywhere for the picking, perhaps because the art of transforming them into a kind of damson jam is lost. I follow the line of the track until I come to a little gated crossing over the line, and here is a surreal sight. The surroundings of the crossing keeper's cottage are festooned with multicoloured gnomes – thousands of them. In a landscape even Disney might find hard to replicate, they are busy fishing, sweeping, gardening, waving and gesticulating with their little staffs, brooms and forks. (The gnomes may be up to all sorts of other things too, for all I know, but I cannot tell since they are crowded into such a congested place.)

'They belong to the widow of the old crossing keeper,' says a dapper man in a railway uniform who darts out of a hut to let me through. 'We call this "Gnome Man's Land Crossing", by the way – you can see why,' he says without any apparent irony. This is Steve, who has one of the quietest jobs on the Wherry Line if not the entire railway network, operating a crossing across the railway which sometimes has only four vehicles a day. This is actually fewer than the number of trains, which run hourly along the line. For this reason, he tells me, the gates are generally set against the road traffic rather than the trains as is standard railway practice. 'On a busy day I may have twenty-five vehicles. But they can't replace me with a machine. Just look at that dangerous curve as the line comes round the bend there.'

With a wave, Steve lets me through the gates on the other side, which open onto a vast seemingly uninhabited area of reed beds, fens, wet meadows, grazing marshes, scrub and woodland, connected by a maze of rivers, dykes and pools – which is the reason for Buckenham station's continued lonely existence. This is the avian kingdom of the Royal Society for the Protection of Birds, and home to some of the major bird sanctuaries of Britain. It may seem bizarre that Buckenham station survives with just five trains each way a week – one on a Saturday and four on a Sunday – but all becomes clear when you realise the trains are strictly for the birds, or those who come to watch them. As if on cue, a honk-ing flock of Egyptian pink-footed geese flies over and, surreally, in this place which with every footstep appears to be a kind of pan-theistic paradise, I bump into a human too. He introduces himself as Tim Strudwick, an RSPB warden, who tells me,

> You should see the marsh harriers here – big birds of prey
> with four-foot wingspans. We've got a big population of
> them. And then we've got the rare bittern, with their deep
> booming voices in the spring. There are only about 150
> bittern overwintering in Britain, so they are very rare. In
> the winter the marshes at Buckenham are alive with the
> sight of huge numbers of widgeon, their white breasts
> glistening like ghosts – maybe 10,000 flying over at a time.

Listening to the cries of the birds on the deserted Buckenham platform with little other prospect than a five-day wait for the next train or a long walk back to Brundall, it is hard to imagine that the Yarmouth and Norwich Railway was once a busy main line, so important that it appointed no less an eminence than George Stephenson as its chairman and his son Robert as engineer. The Stephensons reckoned the line could be completed in eighteen months, but since there were no tunnels or other major bits of civil engineering, it was actually ready in a year. The opening day on 12 April 1844 was an occasion for rejoicing and feasting on a bacchanalian scale. A fourteen-coach train left Norwich with 200 guests, including the Bishop of Norwich, a government inspector and a brass band in the coach next to the engine. The local newspaper reported that 'the electric telegraph having performed its office and informed the manager that all was clear, the engine gave forth its note of warning, the band struck up *See the Conquering Hero Comes*, the engine moved forth in its majestic might . . . the hills reverberated its warning, while the puffs of steam, heard long after its departure, sounded like the breathing of Polypheme.' After a brisk forty-four-minute run and further celebrations, the day concluded with a dinner in the Yarmouth Assembly Rooms, including 'spring chicken, green geese, tongues, pickled salmon, plovers' eggs, ornamental jellies, peaches, strawberries and ices'.

But no time to ponder on such delights. I even have to miss the prospect of exploring Old Buckenham's ancient octagonal-towered All Saints church to power-walk back to Brundall to catch my train to Berney Arms. What is officially Britain's smallest station is rather more copiously provided for than Buckenham, with a generous two trains each way a day. But since it has no electric lights on the platform, the last train leaves well before the evening draws in. I have just seconds to spare when I puff up the footpath into Brundall as Barry is swinging back the big gates to let my train through. From Brundall eastwards, the lines divide, the northern section climbing steeply on a single track to Acle and Yarmouth, contradicting Noël Coward's famous line: 'Very flat, Norfolk.'

The southerly tracks go on to Reedham, where the line splits again – one section going on to Lowestoft and the other swinging north to Yarmouth, via Berney Arms. The views across the flat Broadland as the train heads east are sometimes surreal, with boats seemingly sailing across the fields and fens, an optical illusion created by the river running parallel behind hedges and fences. Sadly, even in our dreams we are unlikely to see many genuine wherries – the square-sailed Norfolk trading barges that have given the line its name. First they were victims of the railways and then of the self-skippered motor cruisers that dominate the Broads, and now there are only two of the original trading wherries remaining. Once there would have been dozens of them bringing beet from the surrounding farms to the huge British Sugar processing plant which dominates the next station at Cantley, with its tall chimney belching exhaust over the neighbouring countryside. Now even the railway doesn't get a look-in. Although there are rusting tracks leading into the factory, where freight wagons would once have brought in beet, coal and limestone and take out sugar and molasses, the last freight train ran in 1988. Now all is carried by lorry, much to the annoyance of local residents. And things may get worse. The Cantley village website complains that new EU rules encouraging the refining of cane sugar in the UK could mean another eighty-five lorry movements a day on the narrow local roads.

But in this sleepy landscape we don't have to worry too much about the impact of industry. Reedham, the next station, is a pretty junction with a timber signal box, old semaphore signals and a chain ferry across the Yare. Here our train leaves the Lowestoft line to take a dead-straight trajectory across the marshes to Berney Arms. It is so squelchy here that the original engineers had to lay down bundles of faggots to prevent the tracks from sinking into the marsh. Make sure you tell the guard you want to get off before the train whizzes past the stop. The platform is just one carriage long and the driver could easily miss it. But why would anyone want to get off at a tiny platform literally in the middle of a seemingly endless marshy void, with no houses in sight and the nearest public road three miles away? One answer is that the local landowner – Thomas Trench Berney, from whom the station takes its name – insisted that the Yarmouth and Norwich Railway should keep services going 'in perpetuity' in exchange for building a station on his land. The alternative answer is better – since Berney Arms is what one writer has described as a 'stepping-off point for an earthly paradise of boundless horizons and reedy dykes'. And silence. Once the train has clattered off into the distance, there is only the sound of a few rooks wheeling overhead and just a whisper of breeze gently brushing the grass. Once there was a small community here. Sheila Hutchinson, a local author, recalls how until the 1940s the railway had a signal box and station cottages that served as the ticket office, waiting room and local post office run by a stationmistress called Violet Mace. Although there was no mains water or electricity, a bell on the wall operated by the signalman would ring across the marshes to announce the arrival of a train. Now there is nothing but grass and sky. The cottages have long been demolished and the current skimpy wooden platform shelter, officially the smallest in Britain, offers all the comforts of an upright coffin. There is a hole cut in the back to prevent the roof from blowing off and to allow the shelter to double as a birdwatchers' hide – not much help in the driving sleet from the North Sea that is typical of a winter's day. And poor Berney Arms station gets no post these days at all.

But wait. Buried among the brambles at the end of the platform is a peeling moss-covered sign that points to BERNEY ARMS MILL. ANCIENT MONUMENT. Cut through a gate, past a swan's nest on a dyke fluorescent with algae, swish through the reeds and there it is, towering over a bend in the Yare: Norfolk's tallest windmill, seven stories high, its cap like an upturned boat hull and its white sails in perfect condition. Although it might appear now as an image of rustic perfection, the original use for the mill was industrial – grinding cement clinker, using clay brought from the Broads by wherry. It was restored to working order by English Heritage in 2007, but the curse of lonely Berney Arms struck again. After the restoration there were never enough visitors coming here to keep it open regularly, and apart from the odd special day it has been closed to visitors ever since. Yet there is one institution in this deserted landscape that still apparently functions – the public house that gives the place its name. Dare I hope the Berney Arms might be open on a quiet lunchtime in the middle of nowhere on an autumn Monday?

A push on a door opposite some skeletal hulks of rotting boats on the riverbank and I am inside a dark wood-lined interior, fragrant with an ancient beery smell of hops and malt. No trendy Norfolk pub this, serving posh seafood to north London second-home owners. Rather, it is a scruffy old boozer stuck in so much of a time warp that I am able to order chicken in a basket without irony. There are few pubs in the land inaccessible except by train (or also by boat in the case of the Berney Arms), and it makes me think of the Adam and Eve, the railway pub described in *Brensham Village,* John Moore's famous book about English village life: 'The stationmaster had his morning and evening pint there, pulling out his great turnip-watch every time a train went by; our only porter spent a great deal of time there as he could afford to do, since the even tenor of his life was interrupted only by four stopping trains a day; and at noon the gangers came in and ordered pints of cider, sat down in the corner with their bait.'

At Berney Arms nowadays of course there is no stationmaster, no porters, nor any staff at all, and woe betide any ganger ordering a cider over lunch. But the landlord, John Ralph, tells me he depends on the railway for his trade, even with the current scorched-earth train service, along with the boaters and walkers who come up from Yarmouth. 'The fact is, there's nobody living round here, so we're a pub without locals – although the occasional farmer pops in for breakfast. The old days, when country people would walk miles to get anywhere, have long gone. It's manic in the summer, but utterly desolate in the winter. And try getting staff. There's just me and the wife – though we've got a Colombian girl in at the moment.' John is a big, bearded Brummie, amply tattooed – a sparks by trade, he tells me, though he looks as though he could have played bass guitar with Meatloaf. He bought the pub after coming here on holiday one summer, although things are not always quite so sunny now. 'We have to go down three miles of local farm tracks to get to the nearest road. Imagine that in the mists we get round here in the winter. One false move and you could go off the road into a dyke. But you'd better get your train. There won't be another along till tomorrow.'

At the station there's just time to admire its single glory, the Indonesian hardwood station sign bearing the name BERNEY ARMS in gunmetal characters. It was made in a local boatyard and installed after the last one got stolen. Somewhere, presumably, there is a back garden masquerading as Britain's smallest station.

I wave down the train back to Reedham and the driver slides open the cab door to let me into the carriage. 'Goodness me, it's rush hour at Berney Arms this afternoon,' he jokes. Even though I already have a return ticket, I splash out on a single to Reedham from the conductor. Around twenty tickets a week are sold to and from Berney Arms each week, so I have done my bit in single-handedly increasing usage by 5 per cent. And in return I get an unusual star-shaped clip in my ticket.

My train from Reedham to Lowestoft runs gently onto the swing bridge across the Yare before heading towards Haddiscoe, where we cross the border into Suffolk. (There's a local joke about a Norfolk man and a Suffolk man standing on the boundary, where a genie asks them both for their wishes. 'My wish is for a high fence all around the county,' says the Norfolk man. 'And mine,' says the Suffolk man, 'is for it to be filled to the brim with water.') Haddiscoe church, which can be seen from the train, is one of the most unusual in England, with a round tower built by the Saxons and a thatched roof. 'The place is so tranquil,' says Simon Jenkins in his book *England's Thousand Best Churches*, 'that we can still imagine the longboats pulled up on the banks of the marsh by what is now the churchyard.' The train is now running upstream along the south bank of the River Waveney, before calling at Somerleyton station, a short distance from Somerleyton Hall, one of the most magnificent Jacobean stately piles in Britain and the home of the Victorian civil engineering entrepreneur Sir Samuel Morton Peto, whose firm constructed the line as well as many buildings in London, including Nelson's column. Charles Dickens was sometimes a guest of Peto here. How much the novelist's time at the hall influenced the writing of *David Copperfield* we cannot know but Copperfield's fictional birthplace at Blundeston (Blunderstone in the novel) is not far from here, and Dickens claimed he chose it after seeing the name on a local signpost.

After the wide-open drama of the marshes, Oulton Broad

North on the last lap into Lowestoft seems disappointingly suburban, though not so disappointing as Lowestoft itself, where the station, constructed by Lucas Brothers, who also built London's Royal Albert Hall, has lost its once-magnificent Baltic timber overall roof, although the walls still stand, giving it the melancholy appearance of a bombed-out church. It is a pity, since a blue plaque on the wall outside proclaims it to be the most easterly station in England and it still retains a large blue enamel sign saying BRITISH RAILWAYS LOWESTOFT CENTRAL, although it is a long time since BR ceased to exist and even longer since Lowestoft had any other stations to confuse it with.

It is a long time too, since holiday trains disgorged thousands here every summer Saturday or loaded fish wagons crossed the road from the docks. In their Edwardian heyday Lowestoft and Yarmouth were among the herring capitals of Europe, landing up to a billion fish a year and dispatching fish trains every hour to London and the Midlands as well as to Harwich for export to Europe. Even the fish waste, processed by hundreds of young women who travelled down from Scotland especially to do the gutting, was dispatched from here – dyed green and destined to be spread on East Anglian fields. The smell is said to have been indescribable.

These days the herring quays are deserted and the fish trains have gone. The produce – mostly shellfish – from the tiny remaining inshore fleet is loaded into the back of vans. Lowestoft's PR people have done a brave job rebranding the town as the capital of the 'Sunrise Coast' although this does not seem persuasive as I wait two hours in the drizzle for my connection to London. Still the 16.58 to Liverpool Street is a train worth waiting for, and the journey over the East Suffolk Line through Beccles, Saxmundham and Woodbridge is one of the great secret treats of the national system.

This is a line that should never, in any logical world, have survived. Although it was once a main line in its own right, it runs parallel to the Great Eastern main line from Norwich through Stowmarket and was thus targeted early by Beeching for closure. Never mind that it was used by crack expresses such as The Easterling – hauled by Sir Nigel Gresley's famous Sandringham Class – it had to go as 'surplus to requirements'. But Beeching did not reckon with the tenacity of the local Suffolk burghers, nor the obduracy of one of his lieutenants, who happened to live along the line. Gerard Fiennes, general manager at the time of the British Railways Eastern Region, believed that Beeching was wrong in his view that rural railways could never pay their way and should thus be eliminated. Why not try simplified signalling, single tracks, pay trains and automated level crossings first? argued Fiennes. (Determination clearly runs in the family, since his relative is the explorer Sir Ranulph Fiennes.) Eventually he was sacked for writing a book called *I Tried to Run a Railway,* which displeased Labour transport minister Barbara Castle, who presided over many of the Beeching closures. But Fiennes's legacy lives on. Mrs Castle reprieved the East Suffolk Line and it thrives to this day on the 'basic railway' principles he espoused, linking sleepy villages, ancient treasures and areas of outstanding natural beauty on its 117-mile route to London.

I've invested in a first-class ticket to sit behind the driver on this modern Turbostar train so I can eavesdrop on the patter as he negotiates our way to Ipswich with the radio-controlled signalling centre at Saxmundham, using virtual tokens issued by a computer rather than the big brass keys or tablets that drivers once had to swap with signalmen to enter single-track sections. (However, the East Suffolk was always double track throughout, with conventional signalling, until downgraded by Beeching into its present mode of operation.) Only three people and a computer are needed to operate the entire line these days, but from my position at the front of the train, this is grand travel indeed, with only seven well-upholstered first-class seats in an exclusive closed-off section, although there are no refreshments, not even a cup of tea in a plastic container from a trolley. With fifteen stations and more than twenty level crossings between here and Ipswich – and pulling into passing loops, to make way for north-bound trains – this is not going to be a fast journey. The trains are slowed down still further by the 'sawtooth' gradients on the line, which was built on the cheap in the 1850s, avoiding cuttings, embankments and bridges wherever possible. This is just as well, since the understated scenery of east Suffolk is best enjoyed at a slow pace.

The line rises from Beccles, plunges into Halesworth and climbs again out of the town on the far side of the River Blyth. These cosy little market towns, off the beaten track, still have a life of their own as centres for the surrounding villages, though once they were junctions for a series of little lines that branched off to the coast. At Halesworth, until 1929 when it shut, you could change for the narrow 3-foot gauge line to Southwold. Passenger services from Saxmundham to Aldeburgh lasted until 1965, long enough to serve the town's most famous resident, Benjamin Britten, on his journeying to and from London. Today it is still open to Leiston for a rather less artistic function – carrying spent nuclear waste from Sizewell power station. At Woodbridge, one of the nicest towns on the East Suffolk Line, the station has been restored and you can almost dip your toes in the River Deben, which laps along the lineside. There are superb views of the town on one side and the estuary on the other. The fabulous gold treasures of the Sutton Hoo ship burial site are located not far from here. Those in search of what is reputedly the best all-day breakfast near the Suffolk coast need look no further than the Whistlestop Café in Woodbridge's old Great Eastern station building, named by the *Guardian* the second-best railway station buffet in Britain.

Before we join the main line at Ipswich there is a long stop, and the driver jumps down from his cab to make an agitated phone call to the signalling centre, with an incantation of numbers and codes. There is a 'failure of lineside equipment', he announces to passengers over the intercom, meaning that we get to Liverpool Street half an hour late. The Grade I-listed building with its magnificent iron roof is the most cathedral-like of the great London termini and is at its most dramatic as dusk is falling. But I ponder on an even bigger marvel than this – that it is possible in the modern age to travel with ease from the smallest station in Britain to the third-busiest. What a score! Berney Arms 1,014 passengers a year; Liverpool Street 57.8 million.

Journey's end: An ex-LNER 'V2' mixed traffic engine
restarts from a signal check at Chester-le-Street, Co. Durham,
with a northbound train in February 1963, the year the station was
slated for closure by Beeching and inspired Flanders and Swann.

CHAPTER TWELVE

THE 07.06 FROM FORMBY – THE STATIONS THAT CAME BACK FROM THE DEAD

Formby to Chester-le-Street, via Southport, Manchester, Stalybridge, Huddersfield, Penistone, Barnsley and Sheffield

No more will I go to Blandford Forum and Mortehoe
On the Slow Train from Midsomer Norton and Mumby Road.
No churns, no porter, no cat on a seat
At Chorlton-cum-Hardy or Chester-le-Street.
We won't be meeting again
On the Slow Train

Funny the way some of the most unpredictable things have the power to resonate through the decades. Even to people who haven't a clue who Beeching was or what he stood for, the name still produces a frisson. 'Doing a Beeching' – there no mistaking the meaning, shorthand for the senseless axing of public services. *Private Eye* magazine still runs a satirical column about the railways called 'Dr B. Ching'. And so it is with some of the words of the comic songwriters Michael Flanders and Donald Swann. This odd couple of middle-aged middle-class men in suits, one in a wheelchair and the other seated at the piano, seem permanently frozen in the black-and-white era of 1950s entertainment. Yet many of their songs have entered the national psyche. Who doesn't remember 'Mud, mud, glorious mud' or 'That big six-wheeler, scarlet-painted, London Transport, diesel-engined, 97-horsepower omnibus'? Or 'Slow Train', written in 1963, the year of the

Beeching report. The song is a litany of some of the poetic-sounding country stations that were due to be closed by Beeching. But it is something more than that. It is an elegy to a vanishing, less-hurried way of British life, and no less resonant now than when it was first written. You can find it on YouTube, and there have been several cover versions, including one adapting the lyrics to the stations on the route of the Orient Express.

In their travelling revue *At the Drop of Another Hat* Flanders and Swann introduced the song thus: 'It's quite a serious song, and it was suggested by all those marvellous old local railway stations with their wonderful evocative names, all due to be axed and done away with one by one, and these are stations that we shall no longer be seeing when we aren't able to travel any more on the slow train.' But, fortunately for us, some of their predictions were wrong. Five of the individual stations mentioned in the song ultimately didn't close. One entire route also escaped the axe. The St Erth to St Ives line, my journey in Chapter 1, stayed open to become one of the most profitable rural branches on the national network. Arram station, between Driffield and Beverley in Yorkshire, survived, as did Ambergate in Derbyshire and Gorton near Manchester (then called Gorton and Openshaw and referred to as Openshaw in the song). How tantalising, then, to take the final journey in this book between the other two survivors, both now busy stations and linked by one of the most beautiful journeys across the Pennines from the western to the eastern sides of northern England. It is difficult to conceive now that either Formby, on the busy Merseyrail suburban network in northern Liverpool, or Chester-le-Street, near Durham, on the East Coast Main Line, which has one of the busiest ticket offices in Britain, could ever have been candidates for closure. And a journey between them is a voyage not just through some of the most diverse landscapes in Britain but across the varied landscape of today's railway system – city and country, ancient and new, jolty old branch lines and restored and reinvigorated modern railways.

This is to be a long journey, on eight trains, so I am up early to join the commuters marching to Formby station in the suburbs of north Liverpool, on the electric City line between Southport and Hunt's Cross. If the station really had closed back in 1963, you might never have noticed its disappearance. It is a modest building partially obscured by a large set of traffic lights on a bridge on the busy road to the shore which thousands of motorists pass each day scarcely giving it a glance, although it's nicely restored with its 1848 red-brick frontage glowing in the morning sun and the original station name and the logo of the old Lancashire and Yorkshire Railway picked out in green and white terrazzo. Scores of folk with briefcases are pouring through the entrance this morning on their way to their Liverpool offices. The Merseyrail system, which runs underground on a loop beneath Liverpool city centre, is the smallest of the national rail franchises, with a track mileage of just seventy-five miles, but is one of the most heavily used in Britain.

Not all my fellow passengers are commuters this morning. In the neat little booking hall with its wooden ticket office picked out in the lemon and white Merseyrail house colours, I queue behind a nun with a group of children in neat convent school uniforms. She is going to Liverpool, she tells me, to see the relics of St Therese of Lisieux, a French nun who died a century ago, whose bones have been doing a tour of Europe and are on display in the cathedral. 'And I've baked some cakes to offer to people waiting to get in. It's good to be neighbourly,' she tells me. Quite right. Because Formby is the heart of middle-class Merseyside. In fact there can be few places in the nation that are more Middle England than this. No tower blocks or sink estates here, just lines of streets with substantial red-brick 'bank manager' semis. Paul Theroux, in his book *The Kingdom by the Sea*, called it a 'land of pink and purple lupins'. Cherie Blair, the former prime minister's wife, claims a proud ancestry in the town, where her great-great grandparents ran a fishing business.

And as my three-car Class 507 unit heads north to Southport, past sand dunes and pines, it only gets posher. The 507s are among the oldest electric trains on the national mainland network and are unique as the only ones outside south-east England to pick up their power from a third rail on the track. Yet they have been nicely refurbished with comfortable seats and you almost feel as though they should have lace antimacassars and net curtains on the windows. Past Freshfield ('Alight for red squirrel reserve') and Ainsdale, nothing could be more suburban than suburban Southport, with the neat greens of the Royal Birkdale Golf Course on both sides of the train. 'Rough Liverpool' is far away as the train reaches the buffers at Southport.

Once this huge station with its eleven platforms (now cut back to six) and great overall roof would have been thronged like its sister Lancashire resorts of Blackpool and Morecambe with holidaymakers from Manchester, Preston, Bolton, and Burnley and beyond. During the 'wakes weeks', when the mills and factories of Lancashire and Yorkshire closed down for their summer holidays and weary sons and daughters of toil headed for the coast on hundreds of excursion trains, Southport was one of the busiest stations in Europe, second only to Blackpool. The novelist Andrew Martin wrote about the enginemen shuttling high-spirited mill workers to the town in his 2005 thriller *The Blackpool Highflyer*: 'The next day, Thursday of Wakes, we were booked for another run to Southport and back. Most of those on the train had already had time away elsewhere earlier in the week and were light-headed with holidayness. There'd been some bottle-throwing from the windows ...' Hard to imagine such behaviour in the genteel Southport of today. Where the booking office and concourse once stood is a giant concrete Marks and Spencer – appropriate for the age profile of its citizens – but it is almost as though the station is longing for busier days again. The extensive sidings built to accommodate the excursion trains are still intact, though weed-grown, as if waiting for wakes weeks to return, the looms to start up in the cotton mills again – and Majorca had not been invented.

Today, Southport station (Chapel Street, as it was once known) seems melancholy indeed, and entirely too grand for the two-car diesel to Manchester on the next leg of my journey; the little train seems tiny and lost in this big terminus. No point hoping to get anywhere else, since services to Preston, the other regional city, so near and yet so far, were withdrawn in 1964 to be replaced by the A565 and A59 roads. 'But some of the trains go to Manchester Airport,' says the man in the orange jacket at the ticket barrier, hopefully, as though I might want to escape Lancashire altogether. In Edwardian times the Lancashire and Yorkshire Railway intro-duced lavishly appointed 'Club' cars on its services to Manchester, where cigar-chomping Mancunian moneymen would breakfast over the *Manchester Guardian* on their way to the office and slurp gin and play poker on the way home. My Pacer train to Manchester Victoria is a world away, with ancient bus seats of the 1970s kind that have mostly disappeared even from buses. It is smoky and wheezy , and the poor suspension of the trains has lent the railway the nickname the 'Rollercoaster Line'. As a result, the locals are not happy. Complaining in the House of Commons, Southport MP John Pugh said, 'I should like a train less than twen-ty years old to arrive in my own town. But I am not holding my breath.' Still, the run through the little villages of the south-west Lancashire plain with their stone-built stations is a reminder of the understated charms of many secondary lines in Britain. Not a lot of guidebook writers or railway enthusiasts come this way, yet the atmosphere is charming in a muted, unsensational fashion. This flat, fertile land was once the larder for Lancashire's great industrial conurbations, and the fields are still there, full of bras-sicas and potatoes. The tangy whiff of fresh celery drifts through the window as we pass through Burscough Bridge. Here the train pulls alongside the Liverpool–Leeds Canal, and a vista of the south Pennines, which I shall cross on my way to my destination at Chester-le-Street, appears black and misty on the distant horizon.

To be fair to Northern Rail, which operates the line, their managers have done much to jolly things up on a limited budget. (Northern has the biggest proportion of loss-making lines of any franchise in the land.) Cheery little Wigan Wallgate makes its modern main line brother on the West Coast Main Line look dreary by comparison. The Victorian porte cochère has been painted a jolly green and red and local people have been encouraged to submit poems to be printed on the windows of the station waiting room. One begins, 'Arrive at the station / Wait for the train / Thought I heard the word cancellation.' If you think that's banal, remember Paul Simon is said to have written the words of 'Homeward Bound' on the platform at nearby Widnes: 'I'm sitting on the railway station / Got a ticket for my destination'.

Cheer doesn't come any more easily in this part of Lancashire than it did in George Orwell's day, and it starts to drizzle as we pass through the drab west Manchester outskirts. Still, it's always a pleasure to arrive at Manchester Victoria, the city's second station and now effectively Britain's capital for slow trains. All the express trains which once ran into its seventeen platforms have long decamped to Manchester Piccadilly and many of the remaining trains that serve the now-downsized Victoria have got even slower. A century ago I could have got here from Southport in forty-five minutes. Today's journey has taken more than an hour.

To the modern eye Manchester Victoria may seem rather scuffed and rundown – at the end of 2009 it was named by the transport secretary Lord Adonis as one of the ten worst stations in Britain. But we must thank our lucky stars that it has survived at all where so many cities have lost their second and third stations to the bulldozer or to other more prosaic uses, such as being turned into supermarkets or warehouses. Goodbye, Manchester Exchange, Glasgow St Enoch, Wolverhampton Low Level, Southampton Terminus, Plymouth Friary, Norwich Victoria,

Lincoln St Marks, Leicester Central, Bath Green Park. The Great Western's once-imposing Birmingham Snow Hill lives on only as a concrete platform under an office block, and Liverpool Central, its impressive cast-iron overall roof gone to the scrapyard, is just a subway station. Lucky indeed are the passengers at Manchester Victoria on their way to Moses Gate or Ramsgreave and Wilpshire. Or to Mytholmroyd, Whalley, Oswaldtwistle, Daisy Hill, Hag Fold or all the other stations with quaint Lancashire names in the Mancunian hinterland that didn't ever close. On their way there, today's passengers still have the chance to admire Manchester Victoria's Edwardian iron and glass canopy bearing the names of the stations the mighty Lancashire and Yorkshire Railway once served from here, now restored after being damaged in the 1996 IRA bombing. Or they may pause to study the L & Y's great tiled mural by the concourse showing the lines that made up its empire while carefully excluding the local routes of all its rivals. The etched glass window bearing the sign 'Gentleman's Lavatory' must be one of the finest surviving in Britain, on or off the railway. Others with time to spare might drop in for a haircut at the Manchester Cutter barber's shop on the concourse, once a regular feature of mainline city termini everywhere – now a rare find and a snip indeed. SUPERB PRECISION HAIRCUT £8, says the sign outside. For the more thrifty, there are CLIPPER CUTS FROM JUST £7.

Choke back those wellsprings of nostalgia, though. Don't shed tears for the halcyon days of the old Lancashire and Yorkshire. There is a far bigger choice for the modern rail traveller than Edwardian Lancastrians might have believed from poring over the company's great tiled map. For the next leg of the journey to Chester-le-Street, there are several magnificent surviving routes across the Pennines. All are united by dramatic climbs, descents and tunnels through the carboniferous limestone of the northern section, and the millstone grit of the southern part. The features they have in common are dramatic, wild moorland scenery and historic industrial towns that formed the cradle of the Industrial Revolution. All have individual character, architecture and charm. I could take a slow train on any of them to my final destination.

Lucky for us, only three of the nine principal trans-Pennine routes running at the time of Beeching have gone. Goodbye to the Cockermouth, Keswick and Penrith line to Darlington (Flanders and Swann mourned the loss of 'Cockermouth for Buttermere') and the Preston to Skipton route via Colne. Beeching wanted to retain the route from Manchester to Sheffield via the great Woodhead Tunnels, newly electrified in 1952, but Margaret Thatcher thought otherwise, and shut it finally in 1981, although passenger services had gone long before. Today though we can still cross the Pennines from Carlisle to Newcastle along the windswept Tyne Valley Line, or take the famous Settle and Carlisle Line, my journey in Chapter 2. The truly adventurous might take the seventy-mile Morecambe to Leeds route, one of the rail network's great secrets (except to the handful of passengers who use its four through trains a day). I could choose the gritty Calder Valley Line from Manchester to Leeds via Halifax, through hard-nosed Yorkshire mill towns such as Hebden Bridge and Mytholmroyd, birthplace of Ted Hughes. Others might be tempted by the quality of the scenery on the Hope Valley Line from Manchester to Sheffield, through the green heart of the Peak District National Park. But how could I resist the most dramatic line of all – from Manchester to Sheffield through Huddersfield and Penistone. Here is excitement unmatched by any of the other lines; it includes a station rated as 'splendid' by John Betjeman as well as a dramatic set of tunnels, the best station buffet on the network and a country railway that has defied closure probably more times than any other.

It's getting towards lunchtime as I leave Manchester Victoria on the hourly train to Huddersfield. With few passengers aboard, the two-coach Pacer is surging like a ship at sea and banging on the track joints like a Bofors gun. Fortunately my journey to

Stalybridge is short. Although it is technically in Greater Manchester, the green shoulders of the Pennines poke prominently into this historic cotton town. Stalybridge is famous for many things. It was the first place where steam power was used in the cotton mills. 'It's a long way to Tipperary' was written here, and the Stalybridge Brass Band is the oldest civilian brass band in the world. Beatrix Potter came from hereabouts and the artist L S Lowry spent his last lonely years in Stalybridge Road, Mottram. But for the hungry (and thirsty) railway traveller there is one claim to fame that eclipses all of these: Stalybridge is widely judged to have the best station buffet in Britain.

Travellers in search of refreshment can't mistake the entrance to Stalybridge station buffet under the huge clock on Platform 1, bearing the legend 'Joyce of Whitchurch'. Next to the door is a blue plaque celebrating its status as the most famous refreshment room on the railway. 'This Victorian Buffet Bar is unique,' it says, 'and is authentic in detail since being rebuilt in 1885.' Lowry did not care for pubs, preferring Kardomah coffee bars, but push open the door and his working-class matchstick men would recognise this place instantly. It's as far away as you can get from the modern station buffet, where bored travellers gulp down flavourless coffee out of styrene cups. Nor could you imagine the cut-glass accents from that other famous station refreshment room at Carnforth in here. Stalybridge station buffet is more the snug at the Rover's Return than *Brief Encounter*.

Queen Victoria stares down from an etched-glass mirror over the marble bar, which glistens with rows of beer pumps. On sale in a glass cabinet on the counter are Werther's Originals and Tunnock's teacakes. This, David the barman tells me, is a favourite place for 'tickers and bottlers' – apparently much the same thing, since tickers collect train numbers and the bottlers keep a tally of the different brands of beer they have drunk. 'Try some of the Nangreaves Crimea,' he urges me. 'It's brewed locally in Bury.' But if feeling abstemious I could have chosen a 'Hot Bovril' or a

'Hot Vimto, 95p' – or a glass of Wincarnis, which according to a notice on the wall, can cure 'brain fag, sleeplessness and mental and physical prostration'. I settle for the beer, along with the 'lunch of the day' – black pudding and black peas. This is quite the largest black pudding I have ever seen, the size of a Greater Manchester police officer's truncheon, and it is fortunate that I have only a few feet to stagger to climb aboard the next train towards Huddersfield.

Once out of Stalybridge, we are climbing hard, the antiquated underfloor bus engine of the train feeling the strain as we ascend through Mossley and Greenfield, on the edge of the Peak District National Park, into the Colne Valley and alongside the Huddersfield Narrow Canal. ('Narrow' equalled cheaper to build, since this is the highest canal in England.) Without notice we plunge into the murk of the Standedge Tunnel, three miles and sixty yards long. Standedge (pronounced Stannige) may be only the third-longest rail tunnel in Britain (after the Severn Tunnel and Totley Tunnel on the Hope Valley Line), but it is certainly the most dramatic, with four parallel tunnels of railway and canal running beneath the high fells. As you might expect, it is drizzling as we enter from Lancashire, but emerging in the West Riding, the sun is skidding across a fluffy sky. Two of the rail tunnels are disused now, but the canal tunnel is an astonishing feat of eighteenth-century engineering – the longest, highest and deepest canal tunnel ever built in Britain. And it's still possible to drive a boat from one end of Benjamin Outram's masterpiece to the other.

I have a hunch that I might be able to climb up to its entrance, and so I get off the train at the next station, Marsden. Everything here is deserted. There are no buildings on the station, no passengers on the train and I pass nobody on the steep road up to the tunnel entrance. There is a pub along the way, but it is shuttered and closed. The empty moors up above, the thin Pennine air, the watery sunshine and some rooks cawing overhead make the scene somehow even more surreal. Around here is some of the emptiest moorland in Britain, including Saddleworth Moor, location of the Moors Murders, where the body of at least one of the child victims of Ian Brady and Myra Hindley has yet to be recovered.

As I approach the tunnel entrance a figure emerges from the darkness of the portal. He turns out not to be a ghost, but a man in a high-visibility jacket who introduces himself as Fred Carter, the tunnel pilot, an occupation that cannot be claimed by many in modern Britain. He tells me the tunnel fell into disuse in 1943 but reopened again in 2001. 'But it's very narrow and there's no towpath. In the old days the boatmen used to "leg" the barges through lying on their backs paddling their feet on the roof. Boats can't pass in there and it can take two hours to get through. I make sure people don't panic in the darkness. If people do get claustro-phobic halfway through, I have a way of getting them out,' he says with a wink. 'There's a boat handy. Fancy a trip?'

Tempting, but I can't take the risk of getting stuck, since I have to get the next train down to Huddersfield, where I have an appointment with a train driver. The journey is only seven miles and I am early into the town, which is famous among other things as the birthplace of Rugby League and the former Labour prime minister, Harold Wilson. The grandeur of the station, however, eclipses both. Built in the Greek style by J P Pritchett in 1846–7, with a huge central block framed by six Corinthian columns and colonnades leading to little pavilions on each side, its magnifi-cence is quite out of proportion to what is only the tenth-biggest town in Britain. Not surprising that Betjeman rated it 'the most splendid station façade in England' and the historian Professor Jack Simmons 'one of those towns where the station is the best building there'. Sadly, Huddersfield has had no direct service to London since the 1950s. Both the station pavilions, which were once booking offices, have been converted into pubs, and inside the Head of Steam, a shrine to railway enthusiasts, its walls covered in signs and nameplates, the barman Kevin says, 'If this station were in bloody London, folk would be slavering over it. It's better than Euston any day. But because it's in Huddersfield, nobody down there gives a toss.' But I wonder whether they really care a lot here either. A gaggle of schoolchildren are larking around by the statue of Harold Wilson in the centre of the splendidly restored George Square outside the station. I ask them who they think it is. Most look blank then one replies, 'Charlie Chaplin.'

But the Grade I-listed station has always had a future, unlike the little branch from Huddersfield to Penistone and Barnsley in South Yorkshire that is the next stage of my journey. Pottering for twenty miles through the *Last of the Summer Wine* country, past remote mining and weaving villages, the Penistone Line has probably come back from the dead more times than any other railway in Britain. Back in 1963 Beeching condemned it, but it was reprieved by Barbara Castle in 1966 because of fears of 'road congestion'. British Railways and the local transport authorities wouldn't give up and there were two more attempts to shut it in the 1980s. But they didn't reckon with the Yorkshire doggedness of people like driver Neil Bentley, who is waiting for me in the cab of the afternoon train in the bay platform to run me down to Barnsley. 'Don't worry, we're very informal round here,' he'd told me the day before when I'd rung to enquire about the services. 'No one's going to mind if you ride in the cab.' Neil is not just a Northern Rail driver, but he's also the chairman of the Penistone Line Partnership, a group of local people who love and defend this railway in the back of beyond with a passion. If there ever was a modern equivalent of *The Titfield Thunderbolt*, then this is it. The line, built by the Lancashire and Yorkshire in 1850, was never anything special in railway terms, though the South Yorkshireman express from Marylebone to Bradford once ran over its tracks. But it has spectacular scenery, jaw-dropping civil engineering and a special place in the iconography of British branch lines as the first on the national network to introduce evening trains as a kind of travelling music hall, with live music and real ale. 'They're mostly packed,' Neil tells me, and I believe him.

Even the train this afternoon – although one of the ubiquitous Pacers – looks rather festive, painted in the jolly crimson livery of the West Yorkshire Metro. Neil, who tells me he is thirty-four and has been with the railway since he was seventeen, presents me with a bottle of their latest gimmick to pack in the passengers – a bottle of Penistone Line Rail Ale, specially produced by the Summer Wine Brewery on the route of the railway near Holmfirth. 'We delivered the first batch to Huddersfield by train and rolled the barrels ceremonially along the platform to the buffet. Sorry about the dirty windscreen,' he says as we pull away from the main line on the wobbly single track down along the Holme Valley. We're joined by Lenny Kinder, the driving team manager, and the men keep up a commentary all the way, a delightful counterpoint between Neil's strong West Riding accent and Lenny's rich Barnsley tones.

Viewed from the cab, the line looks even more rickety since it zigzags from one side of the trackbed to the other – the result of it being singled in the 1980s, the engineers using the bits that were least worn out. 'If there ever was a line that serves its local community then this is it,' Neil tells me. 'There are no buses along much of the route so we're stopping and starting constantly at tiny wayside stations, some only three minutes apart.' Lockwood, Berry Brow, Honley, Brockholes, Stocksmoor, Shepley – all of them sleepy little stone-built villages thankful that their stations never closed.

We cross the 121-foot Lockwood Viaduct and Lenny gives a parp on the horn. 'That's for his missus, who lives up on the hill,' says Neil. 'He always gives a toot to let her know he's passing by.' This was once prime textile country. Streams have always poured down the valley sides, draining the high moorland, providing soft water for washing the wool and powering the mills. Then the

Industrial Revolution came along and what was once a cottage industry was turned into sixty smoking mills, all within a stone's throw of here. All are now closed or changed to more modern uses, and these days the local mill may well be a graceful converted home for well-off commuters to Sheffield or Leeds.

Brockholes used to be the junction for the branch to Holmfirth, once famous across Britain for Bamford's, publishers of the saucy seaside postcards of Donald McGill, but more recently as the setting for *Last of the Summer Wine,* now in the history books as the BBC's longest-running sitcom. I peer out of the cab window to see if Compo or Nora Batty are getting aboard, but the train crew are busy telling me about badgers. 'The second-biggest badger ever recorded was found round here,' says Lenny. 'And we see lots of tawny owls too,' says Neil. We pass some signs by the track pointing out that this is a Site of Special Scientific Interest because of the badgers hereabouts. 'Barmy to advertise it,' says Lenny. 'There's nothing they like better down in Barnsley than a bit of badger baiting.'

Yet there is much to boast about as we head south towards Barnsley, the men talking over the constant *ping* of the train's automatic warning system. Here is the station at Denby Dale, famous for its monster pies, baked for special occasions – the first in 1788 to mark King George III's recovery from madness, and the most recent baked for the Millennium, weighing 12.52 tonnes. Then onto the dramatic Penistone Viaduct, higher and with more arches than even the celebrated Ribblehead Viaduct on the Settle and Carlisle Line. 'S & C fans hate it when I point out to them that our viaduct is better,' says Neil. Penistone has its own claim to fame as reputedly the coldest town in Britain, but it doesn't stop cinema fans flocking there to hear the mighty Compton organ at the Penistone Paramount, one of the last working cinema organs in Britain.

The Penistone line ends at Barnsley station, now blandly called Barnsley Interchange, and as I wait for the next train north to

Leeds I wonder what its plain-speaking sons Michael Parkinson and Arthur Scargill would make of such an uninspiring place. I have no regrets about leaving Barnsley, but I am sorry to say good-bye to what must be the friendliest line in Britain as I head along the main line to Sheffield, where I change for my final destination at Chester-le-Street, just north of Durham on the London to Edinburgh main line.

Although Chester-le-Street, an ancient town on the Roman road to the north and famous as the home of Durham County Cricket Club, eluded Beeching's axe, it survived with just a sprinkling of trains. All the fast London to Newcastle and Edinburgh expresses hurry through without stopping and there is a big gap in the middle of the day with not much of a service at all. But it does sport a real-life 'station master' in the form of Alex Nelson, who is waiting to greet me on the platform. At least, 'Station Master' is what it says on his business card, which is printed on what appears to be a platform ticket.

'Welcome,' he declares, 'to the centre of Britain' – perhaps an odd way of describing this out-of-the-way corner of rural Durham. But Alex, it turns out, is no eccentric throwback to the old days of the railway, nor is he really a stationmaster. Instead, he runs one of the most successful independent railway ticket agencies in Britain, having rescued Chester-le-Street station, with its charming North Eastern Railway buildings, by making it his headquarters. His claim to be at the centre of Britain is based on his ownership of the Internet domain name nationalrail.com, which he snaffled perfectly legally in the 1990s from under the nose of the newly privatised railway. Now, he explains, anyone who goes on the Internet to buy a ticket may well find themselves – virtually– at Chester-le-Street station instead of the National Rail website. 'People are mystified about the pricing of railway tickets and haven't a clue what the best deals are, so my staff (he has five working for him) talk them through it,' he tells me over a mug of tea in his bustling booking office. So what's his best tip?

'Book in advance. And go first class,' he says. 'A standard single from Newcastle to Durham costs three pounds. But if you pay £4.50 to go first class, you don't only get a comfy seat, you get a ploughman's lunch, a coffee and a newspaper thrown in with the price. Not bad, huh?

'I'll tell you something else that many don't know,' he says. 'The Bible was first translated into English here in Chester-le-Street.' He whisks me across the main street to the parish church of St Mary and St Cuthbert, and like the stationmasters of old, who were once pillars of their communities, Alex receives many a wave and a handshake from the local people, who seem to know him well. In a glass cabinet in the darkness of the church is a replica of the magnificent illuminated manuscript of the Lindisfarne Gospels, one of the great treasures of world literature, brought to Chester-le-Street in the ninth century by monks fleeing from Holy Island, where it was originally made. (The original also reposes next to a railway station – in the British Library at St Pancras in London.) Between the lines of Latin, in a neat Anglo-Saxon hand, is the translation made by Aldred, provost of Chester-le-Street, more than a millennium ago – the very first rendering of the Bible into English.

'What we do in the booking office at the station now,' Alex Nelson says, 'is exactly what the monks were doing back in the tenth century. Making complicated things accessible to ordinary people.'

FURTHER READING

One of the joys of travelling round the country on slow trains is the opportunity to browse in second-hand bookshops while waiting during sometimes-long gaps in the service. As a result I have bought far too many obscure books on old railways than are good for anyone with already-groaning bookshelves. So I will mention only the essential ones here.

S K Baker, *Rail Atlas Great Britain and Ireland* 12th edition (OPC 2010)

Gordon Biddle and O S Nock, *The Railway Heritage of Britain* (Michael Joseph 1983)

Ian Carter, *British Railway Enthusiasm* (Manchester University Press 2008)

Jonathan Glancey, *John Betjeman on Trains* (Methuen 2006)

C Hamilton Ellis, *The Trains We Loved* (George Allen & Unwin 1947)

Alexander Frater, *Stopping Train Britain* (Hodder & Stoughton 1983)

Brian Hollingsworth, *The Pleasures of Railways* (Allen Lane 1983)

Alan Jowett, *Jowett's Railway Atlas of Great Britain and Ireland* (Patrick Stephens 1989)

Miles Kington, *Steaming through Britain* (Unwin Hyman 1990)

David McKie, *Great British Bus Journeys* (Atlantic Books 2006)

Bryan Morgan (ed.), *The Railway Lover's Companion* (Eyre & Spottiswoode 1963)

Michael Pearson, *Iron Roads to the Isles; Iron Roads to the Broads and Fens* (Wayzgoose 2001, 2005)

Harold Perkin, *The Age of the Railway* (Panther 1970)

Michael Robbins, *The Railway Age* (Routledge & Kegan Paul 1962)

Jack Simmons, *The Railways of Britain* (Routledge & Kegan Paul 1961)

David St John Thomas, *The Country Railway* (David & Charles 1976)

Paul Theroux, *The Kingdom by the Sea* (Houghton Mifflin 1983)

Christian Wolmar, *Fire and Steam* (Atlantic Books 2007)

More detailed literature will be found in the lists and back catalogues of the following publishers: Ian Allan, David and Charles, the Oakwood Press, the Oxford Publishing Company and the Middleton Press. One of the best selections of out-of-print books on railways can be found appropriately at the unspoilt railway station at Stamford in Lincolnshire, where the slow trains continue to stop and the booksellers, Robert Humm and Co. occupy the former booking office.

ACKNOWLEDGEMENTS

Special thanks to Paul Bigland, Rupert Brennan-Brown, Patrick Janson-Smith, Brian MacArthur, Chris Milner, Melanie Powell, Marcus Robertson and Hassard Stacpoole for their inspiration and encouragement in writing this book; to my publisher Trevor Dolby for suggesting the idea and my agent Sheila Ableman for keeping me on the right track. I'm very grateful also to Paul Bigland, Chris Milner and Anthony Lambert for reading the manuscript and for their expert suggestions and additions, and to Michael Ward of the University of Central Lancashire for providing study leave to ensure the project was finished speedily and is thus as up-to-date as possible. All errors are obviously mine.

Writing about railways is necessarily a minefield, since so intense is the British national passion for trains, there will always (rightly) be someone, somewhere who knows better than me. I'd be delighted to receive comments and corrections, which may be sent to mwmedia.uk@gmail.com, bearing in mind that I have tried to convey a reporter's view of travelling on Britain's rail network in 2009 rather than to produce a detailed historical or technical account. There are many of these in existence already, which are infinitely more detailed than anything achievable within the scope of this book – although often somewhat drier in tone.

Thanks too to Steven Knight of Virgin Trains for his generous support and faith in the book, as well as Sue Evans of First Great Western, John Gelson and Peter Meades of National Express, Emma Knight of South West Trains and Iain Wilson of First ScotRail. I have had invaluable help from Neil Buxton and his enthusiastic staff and volunteers at the Association of Community Rail Partnerships. There are others too numerous to mention, but I owe the biggest debt to the hundreds of ordinary passengers and railway staff I met on trains and railway stations during thousands of miles of travel between the early spring and late autumn of 2009, who took the time to chat and share a little bit of their lives with me. Without the 'kindness of strangers' this book could never have been written.

LIST OF ILLUSTRATIONS

INDEX

medicines and what belongs to other social practice areas must be placed somewhere, but where?

The legal framework in which alternative medicine is situated

When applied to the practice of alternative medicines, the legislative bases of the health system in France generate a series of ambiguities and paradoxes. They are extensively due to the fact that official recognition of different medicines is primarily part of an action of legitimation (or of non-legitimation) by such and such an authority, and in reality has little to do with actually being entered into the laws applying to the different categories of players and of institutions concerned. Thus, while homoeopathy, and to a lesser extent acupuncture, are disciplines whose validity is still being contested by the Academy of Medicine, prescriptions or medical consultations to which they give rise are codified and reimbursed by the Social Security and have been for several years and are thus blessed by their backing.

Similarly, no alternative therapy (including the most widespread acupuncture; homoeopathy, phytotherapy, osteopathy), is the subject of teaching at a national level. Except for the DUMENAT (Diplôme Universitaire de Médicines Naturelles), issued by a university in the Paris area (Bobigny), there are no officially recognised qualifications in the field. Indeed, certificates or diplomas for homoeopathy or acupuncture, issued by certain medical faculties, are not considered as official national diplomas. Obviously, the same applies to diplomas issued by a great many private schools. However, any doctor can declare himself to be a homoeopath or an acupuncturist, regardless of any additional training he may or may not have followed.

More generally, in France there is a two-fold movement as far as the legitimation of the practice of alternative medicine is concerned, at doctors' level. First, there is a loosening up, or even an opening up, by most of the official authorities (medical professional organisations, faculties of medicine, Ministry of Health, etc) with respect to these doctors. Second, there is greater vigilance, in particular among the medical profession, regarding the conditions under which these medicines are applied and the struggle against medical charlatans (even within the medical profession), regarding prescriptions for natural therapies in the case of serious illness for instance. This vigilance is becoming apparent through the increased number of appearances of doctors before disciplinary boards. From the legislative standpoint, the keystone is the freedom that the doctor is legally entitled to in prescribing therapy that he considers appropriate to the case being dealt with.

However, alternative medicine in France is practised not only by doctors. The main legal problem that arises is due to the fact that doctors have a monopoly for exercising medicine (drawing up diagnosis and decisions regarding therapeutic behaviour). However, many non-doctors, in particular kinesiotherapists, have been trained in non-orthodox therapies and claim the right to practise acupuncture, osteopathy and other alternative therapeutic disciplines. The fact that there is no official regulation concerning acupuncturists, osteopaths, naturopaths etc. forms a legal loophole giving a great deal of the European market dispositions which should come into effect in 1992. For their part, doctors – acupuncturists and osteopaths in particular – are very actively organising matters to deal with such claims and to ensure a monopoly for the distribution of alternative care.

Number and characterists of therapists

Because there is no regulation concerning alternative medical 'specialities', the number of practitioners cannot be evaluated with any accuracy. This is particularly so in the case of non-doctor therapists.

Several estimates agree on the number of acupuncturist doctors as approximately 10,000, while the number of homoeopathic doctors is between 3000 and 6000; the number of osteopaths estimated as between 150 and 300. Among them, is there any reason to distinguish between doctors who make exclusive or majority use of these therapies and those who implement them more occasionally?

According to a survey in 1987[5] taken from a specimen range of 200 general practitioners, 36% of the doctors investigated declared that they practised one or several alternative methods (in France in 1987 there were 54,500 general practitioners working on an independent basis); of these 46%, 5.4% used them exclusively, 20.7% used them often, 72.8% used them occasionally (no answer: 1.1%). Approximately one GP in four cares for his patients regularly by alternative therapies. Other soundings give similar results.

Doctors using unorthodox therapies are for the very greater part general practitioners. An increasing number of pediatricians (even if this is still a minority) are turning toward homoeopathy and some rheumatologists are becoming interested in acupuncture or manual medicines. Sophrology appears to be having some success among dentists and midwives.

The number of kinesiotherapists using alternative therapies can be estimated as between 2000 and 4000 (out of 25,700 kinesiotherapists working on a freelance basis).

It is thought that the number of practitioners who have no official diploma as a health professional – among whom there are many naturopaths – is even more difficult to evaluate; it must be around several thousand.

The type and length of training of these therapists, doctors or non-doctors appear to vary greatly. Some (perhaps the great majority?) have very solid training, while others are far less well equipped. It should be observed that in particular, as far as osteopathy and acupuncture are concerned, some practitioners declare that they were trained on the 'compagnonage' basis (ie. by working with a qualified and experienced practitioner). This type of apprenticeship may or may not be a complement to more 'scholarly' training[6].

The number of schools and training courses in alternative medicines has increased substantially over the last 15 years or so. Alongside the 'benchmark' schools which obtain their letters of legitimacy in the field of different medicines (even if the diplomas they issue are not officially recognised), many more or less 'serious' training centres have been founded.

More generally, the field of different medicines in France is strongly structured and institutionalised. One important point to be emphasised is that the major therapeutic and heterodox disciplines (acupuncture, homoeopathy, phytotherapy, osteopathy) do not form consistent wholes. Within each of these medicines there are doctrinal splits which extend the institutional splits that exist (among the unions of practitioners, training schools, knowledgeable societies, etc).

In France, much research has been devoted to practitioners of different medicines on the basis of original data collections (surveys by questionnaires or by conversations). This work forms part of what we might well call the sociology of the health professions; a study of the professional and social trajectories, positioning on the care market (choice of practising conventional or fee-free systems), doctrinal and therapeutic orientations, relations with professional groups (unions, knowledgeable companies, etc), methods of legitimisation through the acquisition of knowledge, by 'donation', by reference to major cultural traditions, etc.

One very interesting area of research consists of